1. 00

# BICKERS

# BICKERS

THE AUTOBIOGRAPHY OF
**Martin Bicknell**

FOREWORD BY
**Alec Stewart**

GreenUmbrella
Publishing

This edition first published in the UK in 2008
By Green Umbrella Publishing

© Green Umbrella Publishing 2008

www.gupublishing.co.uk

Publishers: Jules Gammond and Vanessa Gardner

Creative Director: Kevin Gardner

Picture Credits: Getty Images and Martin Bicknell

Printed and bound by J. H. Haynes & Co. Ltd., Sparkford

ISBN: 978-1-906229-65-8

For family and friends

# Contents

Starting Out                                                    1

Surrey and Turning Pro                                         10

Early Years                                                     23

On the Fringes of England                                      36

Back to Surrey                                                  50

Test Call-Up At Last                                           62

Barren Times                                                   74

Success At Last                                                87

The Long Wait is Over                                         104

No Call-Up, More Trophies and Tragedy Again                  120

England Call Again                                            135

Implosion and Steve Rixon – A disastrous Two Years           149

The End is Nigh                                               163

Ball Tampering                                               175

The English Game                                             190

What Now?                                                    201

**Martin Bicknell**

# Foreword by Alec Stewart

Jack Hobbs, Alec Bedser, Stuart Surridge, Peter May and Ken Barrington are just some of the greats that have represented Surrey CCC over the years, and I don't think anyone would mind if I added to the list the name of Martin Bicknell. When Bickers started off his career as a young and very promising swing bowler no one could have predicted just how big a contribution he would make to Surrey cricket. It is not often that I am immediately impressed, but this young man made his mark on me as soon as he began his professional career. He bowled with decent pace and had the natural ability to swing the ball – an art that is dying in the modern game – while maintaining excellent control of his line and length, and was a good listener as he aimed to improve on his all round game. Geoff Arnold, his bowling mentor, played a huge part in his development and it is no coincidence that their bond is still as strong as ever. Bickers' bowling record is outstanding and, but for injuries and the England selectors' desire for genuine pace bowlers, I am convinced that he would have had a long and successful International career. When he "retired" from Test cricket, in the same game as I did against South Africa on our home

# BICKERS

ground at The Oval in 2003, he will have looked back and wondered if he deserved more than his four caps. I will not be in the minority when I say he could and should have had a minimum of 50 caps to his name, when you consider he was first selected to go on the Ashes Tour of 1990/91.

Bickers should not be too depressed with his lack of caps as he knows just how much respect he has earned from all those that have played against him and how highly he is thought of. The Surrey success of the late 1990s early 2000s was due, in no small measure, to Martin's all round contribution. By this time he had developed into a genuine all rounder, making telling contributions with the bat while regularly removing the opposing top order without fuss. Adam Hollioake, the Surrey captain at the time, knew that when the going got tough, Bickers would step up to the plate and perform. Like all good opening bowlers he believed that the game of cricket was always in the batsmen's favour and that the bowlers were hard done by. As you can imagine, us batters took great delight in telling him otherwise, while reminding him that if a batsman makes a mistake more times than not his innings is over while a bowler has so many more opportunities to make up for the bad ball!! He would have none of this, and many a dressing room discussion would centre around Bickers and his theories on the game!

As time went by and he became the senior voice of the dressing room, he was always keen to have his say on anything and everything, and in his eyes he was always right! A more popular member of a team you will not find, and whether he was offering advice or leading by example out on the field, Bickers was always the consummate professional. I would like to think that any young player who has spent time in his company will have

# Martin Bicknell

learnt from the great man and realised that hard work and dedication to your profession pays off. He certainly learnt a lot from playing with the likes of Sylvester Clarke and Waqar Younis, and though he never had their pace he was able to pick up things that helped improve his bowling, whether it be the use of the bouncer or the art of reverse swing. By the end of his playing time Bickers was the complete bowler, and as much as I hate to admit it, it was a pleasure to watch him purvey his trade. As a wicket keeper you always knew that an edge would be coming your way and it was then your job to hang on to the catch as I promise you, from experience, if you dropped it he would never let you forget it! I once dropped the prolific Jimmy Cook while playing against Somerset at Weston Super Mare in the mid 1990s when he was on 14 and he went on to get a big hundred. I have to admit that it was the easiest catch I dropped in my career, and to this day Bickers still goes on about it!!!

I am sure that this book will give you a true insight into his wonderful life as a Surrey cricketer as well as his time away from the cricket field, but all I can add is that it was a great privilege to have seen him develop from a schoolboy cricketer into the finished article, and to count him not just as a team mate but a true friend as well. A Surrey legend he most certainly is and I suggest that anyone looking to make their way in the great game of cricket takes on board what Bickers has to say. He may have finished playing but I hope that he will be in a position to pass on his wisdom to the next generation of cricketers. Congratulations on a fine career, I just hope this book is more interesting than listening to him drone on about his beloved football team, Leeds United!!!!!

# Starting Out

There I was, standing at the end of my run-up; a full house at The Oval, a Test match and me bowling. I knew what I had to do. Jacques Rudolph, the South African middle order batter, had just left two outswingers alone outside the off stump. So there was only one thing for it. I fixed the ball in my hand and rehearsed in my mind what I wanted to do. I started my run-up and told myself to keep my wrist behind the ball, to get the line right and pitch it up; hopefully the ball would do the rest. The ball came out beautifully, a perfect line. Rudolph, thinking it was another ball slanted across him, started to shoulder arms. The arc of the ball started to shape back towards the stumps. I knew what was about to happen and so did he. As the ball swung back to hit the top of off stump, it was as if everything I had worked for, everything I had dreamt of as a kid, growing up playing back-yard cricket, dreaming of greater glory, had fallen into place. The deafening roar of that Sunday afternoon crowd told me I had succeeded; I was good enough to play for England. I was helping England to win a Test match, not in Normandy where I first learnt to play the game, but my professional back yard, The Oval.

That moment encapsulated my whole career. I was a skilful bowler, able to deceive batsmen and bowl to any situation, but I lacked that extra yard of pace in many people's eyes. The ball that hit the top of Jacques

Rudolph's off stump didn't knock the stump out of the ground as most fast bowlers' deliveries would have done. It knocked it back half way. It was as if the stump was saying something to me. "You were good enough to hit me, but you are not quick enough to knock me out of the ground."

Shortly after the Test match finished, so had my international career. It was another fleeting visit to the international stage, but this time I walked away knowing I could stand in the highest company. I was now too old to consider a run in the side. I had done my job, brought back to give a little control and skill to the England pace attack. We won the last Test and secured a drawn series. Everyone was happy.

I grew up sports mad; I still am. I love the live action of a top sports event. I love competing and testing myself. I was lucky to have an older brother, Darren, to share my love of all things sporting. We paired off against each other, always fighting it out, whether it was me bowling at him in the back garden, or the two of us playing Subbuteo football on the dining room table. And we were also very lucky to have parents to support us in all we did. Not that it was easy. My father left my Mum before I was born. They were very young and he couldn't handle the situation. It left my Mum very much on her own until I was four, when she met my step-father, Vic. They married and gave us stability at home, and I will always think of Vic as my father. I finally met my paternal father, Melvin, when I was 30. I had always wanted to meet him, but never found the right time. I didn't hold a grudge for what happened. It was all water under the bridge for me.

We lived in a variety of places – with my Grandmother in Godalming, Normandy, Littlehampton and Bognor Regis before finally coming back to live in Ash, just outside Guildford, where I was born. My love of sport probably started from the age of five when, realising there were no local football teams worth supporting, I chose Leeds United. It was right at the end of the Don Revie era and Leeds were the best team in the country. It was an easy decision. Darren chose West Ham. I thought they were rubbish, and the countless hours of arguing about which was the better team kicked off. Needless to say he has had the better of the argument in recent years.

The love of live sport started with my uncle. A lifelong Southampton supporter, he took the pair of us all over the country to follow his team. We developed a bit of a soft spot for the Saints. Some memories never fade, like Mick Channon wheeling away after scoring a goal, or standing on the terraces with the smell of hot Cornish pasties and cigarette smoke wafting up our nostrils. My first Leeds game was at Arsenal. I think my uncle got bored with me carping on about Leeds being the best side in the world, so he took me to prove they weren't. A very dull 0-0 draw proved he was probably right.

We were both heavily into cricket from an early age. I remember Dennis Amiss scoring a double hundred against the might of the West Indies at The Oval in 1976, and Michael Holding ripping through the England batting line-up twice. We went on the day that was ruined by rain so we only saw a few overs bowled. The following year we got Vic to take us up to the Oval again, this time to watch England v Australia. It was a place that would become very much part of our future. It seemed massive. We sat side on and tried to follow the ball down the pitch – to no avail. It all happened so fast – Dennis Lillee, hair flapping in the wind as he sprinted in to bowl, Ian Botham taking the last wicket of the day and Derek

# Martin Bicknell

Underwood fielding in front of us. We were officially hooked on cricket.

By the time we were 9 and 10 we had to find a club to play for. School cricket was virtually non-existent, so Normandy Cricket Club became our second home. We loved it – the warm summer nights, a field full of boys playing cricket and the smell of freshly cut grass. Our first cricket coach, Bernard Hobbs, taught us the basics of the game, and we spent the rest of our time practising. We couldn't get enough. School holidays meant one thing. If we weren't watching the cricket on the TV we were outside playing it. We would organise games between our mates or play just the two of us. We lived and breathed cricket. Of course it wasn't just cricket. The winter meant football, and we approached that in a similar way. Darren was always a goalkeeper and I was a striker, so we had the perfect match. For hours we played football outside the house, and if it was raining we played in the house, much to Mum's annoyance.

I must have made an impression on someone with my cricketing prowess. My first representative game of cricket came when I was 10. Along with Graham Thorpe and Shaul Udal, I represented Surrey Under 10s in a 20-over game near Camberley. I have no real recollection of what happened in the game, just that it obviously didn't go that well as I didn't play again for another year. Even then, I only played one game for the Surrey Under 11 side as I made a relatively slow start. It wasn't until I was 12 that I became a regular in the Surrey setup. Graham Thorpe was the star of the show; we were all in his shadow. He would bat number three and score runs for fun, which meant batting number four could be a long waiting game. At least I opened the bowling. I started making a bit of a name for myself with a good action and decent performances. Cricket coaching courses followed under Surrey's Nescafé coaching programme and I was well and truly into the 'system'.

It was time to say goodbye to Normandy. I felt I had to go to a bigger club and as Guildford were the biggest around that's where I wanted to be. I wanted more cricket. Guildford played mid-week matches against local sides and with better facilities and pitches than Normandy it was an easy decision to make. Under the guidance of Brian Ruby, Darren and I both developed at a good rate, and were both playing men's cricket on Saturdays before too long.

Although I was shaping up as a pretty useful sportsman, school was a different matter. Since we travelled around the south of England before we settled in Ash, I had been to a variety of schools, none of which I really settled in. South Ash Middle School became my first settled school. After middle school I moved on to the more imposing Robert Haining Secondary. Robert Haining was nearly four miles from where we lived and as we were in possession of new bikes it meant we had to cycle to and from school. It wasn't a lot of fun but I guess it strengthened my legs no end. School seemed to pass me by quite fast. So obsessed was I with sport that my education definitely took a back seat. I tried pretty hard, always did my homework but I didn't grasp what was required quickly enough to get a decent set of exam results. My thoughts were never far from sport and if I wasn't playing it I was watching it. If I wasn't doing either of those things I was dreaming about it. I sure put myself under plenty of pressure to play cricket for a living. But it wasn't just cricket I wanted to play. Football was every bit as much a part of my life and I dreamt of playing for England, of running out at Wembley, scoring the winning goal and lifting the World Cup. Alas, no real recognition came quickly enough and my focus became cricket. Doors began to open.

I progressed well through the Surrey age group sides. It was a fairly bizarre system though. One year would be under the Surrey Schools' banner and the next year would be under the Surrey Cricket Association. The result was that from year to year the sides could change dramatically. The Surrey Schools' system was very political and leant very heavily on the private schools for its players. Graham Thorpe and I were the only kids from secondary schools and the standard of the other boys was pretty poor to say the least. There were far too many favours going on to satisfy the headmasters of certain schools and our performances suffered as a result. If Graham or I had an off day, there was no one else capable of coming up with any sort of performance. Fortunately, by the time we reached the Surrey Young Cricketers side, the practice of picking boys based on which school they went to had died off. The team was run expertly by Mike Edwards, a former Surrey player who really knew his stuff at this level.

My performances for Surrey Under 15s were deemed good enough to make it to the English Schools' Festival and represent the South of England. I had taken a record number of wickets for Surrey and headed off to the Festival in good shape. However it turned into a bit of a disaster. I opened the bowling and, feeling really nervous for the first time in my cricketing life, I froze. I bowled pretty poorly throughout the three games I played. In one game I bowled just the one over before being taken off. In the last game, against the North of England, I did at least bowl one decent spell to salvage a little pride. I knew I hadn't done anything like enough to make it into the full England Schools side so it didn't come as a major shock when they announced the side at the end of the tournament and I discovered that I hadn't been selected. What was a shock was when Graham Thorpe's name was read out, as a bowler! Graham had hardly bowled throughout the tournament and I had outperformed him all summer with the ball. My problems with the selectors were just starting so it seemed.

Back in Surrey colours things were really on the up and up. As a 16-year-old, I was playing for the Surrey Young Cricketers, an Under 19 team, and performing pretty well. I was selected to go to the Cambridge Festival as part of a nationwide competition for counties and some minor counties. I was very much the youngster in the team and being young and naive was led astray pretty easily. Boys on tour tend to find themselves involved in a little mischief from time to time and this trip was no exception. One evening we ended up in a bar in the middle of Cambridge where we sampled most of the top shelf. As I was the youngest, I was easy prey, and was stitched up royally. We played drinking games, where it appeared I was the only one who didn't know the rules. I drank more in one night than I had in my whole life up until that point. Needless to say the next morning I couldn't have felt any worse and I had a day's cricket ahead of me. How I got through it was a bit of a mystery and I even seemed to evade being detected by the management. It was a good job they didn't smell my breath. As for the tournament, we got through to the semi-finals before being knocked out by Middlesex. Before the match, while our warm-ups and fielding drills were taking place, I witnessed one of the worst accidents I have seen on a cricket field. It was a really windy day and Mike Edwards was hitting catches. Darren took off at full pace to get under a sky-high ball but there was a problem. In his way there was a sightscreen and he was haring straight at it. He couldn't hear the warning shouts above the wind and he hit the side of the sightscreen full on. If it wasn't so serious it would have been hilarious. It was like a scene out of a cartoon where the bad guy is knocked clean out running into a wall. Except this time Darren lay on the grass with a fractured cheek bone and a pool of blood in his eye. It was horrible. We didn't exactly set the world alight with our performance after that, and were on our way home. Well – not all of us. Darren stayed in Cambridge and underwent an operation to insert a steel plate into his face and missed the rest of the season. He wasn't best pleased.

I knew Surrey were interested in signing me. They were going through a bit of a transition and were about to release a couple of seam bowlers off the staff. With gaps appearing in the squad I knew my opportunity could be imminent. I got selected to play in a Second XI game at The Oval against Middlesex. It was a three-day match, something I had not experienced before, and playing at a level way above Surrey Under 16 cricket but I coped pretty well. I had good control, even at that age, and swung the ball away from the bat. I took seven wickets in the match and followed that up with good performances in some one-day matches. I was young though and very much out of my depth in such a grown-up environment. Fortunately I had Geoff Arnold, who was running the 2nd XI, guiding me through everything I did. He took me to most of the matches and we would talk cricket all the time. I had a lot to learn and he was the perfect teacher.

# BICKERS

Towards the end of the season came the moment every boy dreams about. Mickey Stewart took me to one side at Banstead Cricket Club during a Surrey Young Cricketers match and told me I was to be offered a two-year contract. I was so excited I didn't even bother to find out how much I was getting paid. The £100 a week barely mattered to me. I was a professional cricketer. I had finally made it.

# Surrey and Turning Pro

At last my dream had come true. On 1st April 1986 I realised my ambition and became a professional cricketer. I approached my new career with a feeling of excitement and trepidation. Was I good enough to play at this level? What do I do if it doesn't work out? What will the senior players think of me? I have never been the most confident of people, despite what some people think and this would put me to the test. I felt like a fish out of water, 17 years old and distinctly green behind the ears.

It was a bit of a surreal feeling, walking through the gates as a professional for the first time. I was actually getting paid for something I would willingly have done for nothing. All my other mates were either at college or getting their first jobs too. If I hadn't become a professional cricketer I haven't a clue what I would have done with myself. I guess that was all the incentive I needed to make it work. The hunger and the desire to succeed were accentuated because of the position I had put myself in as a result of my school work (or lack of it). Maybe it wasn't a bad thing. I had nothing to fall back on – so this had to work out.

In those days there were still two Surrey dressing rooms – one for the capped players and one for the young lads. I was assigned my changing area and a small locker for what little kit I had. Next to me was Keith Medlycott, a young left-arm spinner who would go on to manage the first team later in my career. Medders was a larger than life character and made me feel very welcome. Also in that dressing room were David Ward, Mark Feltham, Richard Doughty and Nick Falkner, along with the new boys – me, Jonny Robinson and Graham Brown, a young wicket-keeper from Balham. Alec Stewart had just graduated to the first-team dressing room but spent most of his time coming back into our room. He, too, was to play a huge part in helping me settle in my early career. The first-team dressing room was an intimidating place. Basically, as a young lad, it was out of bounds to me and to be honest I didn't really fancy it anyway. All I saw was a miserable bunch of cricketers in a smoke-filled dressing room. It was best to keep out.

In charge of the whole operation were Mickey Stewart and Geoff Arnold. Mickey had managed the Surrey Under 18 tour to Australia a few months prior to me joining the staff so I knew him fairly well. Geoff Arnold was a no-nonsense coach who called a spade a spade, and over the course of the next 10 years at the club he would have the biggest influence on my career. There were all sorts of stories circulating about Arnold and his run-ins with several of our players. In a second-team match at Guildford the previous year, Nick Taylor, a seam bowler who had just left the club, had politely enquired when they were getting paid. Unfortunately for Nick his timing wasn't great; Surrey had just lost and he received the mother of all bollockings from Arnold. Nick soon found himself pinned up against the dressing-room wall with a Duncan Fearnley bat wedged under his chin. Needless to say Nick was a little unconcerned about his next pay packet after that incident. As a young man, Arnold put the fear of God into you, and getting on the wrong side of him was not a good idea.

# Martin Bicknell

It was almost a relief to get out onto The Oval and play some cricket. I felt pretty uncomfortable in the dressing-room environment. I struggled with the constant piss-taking and I wasn't confident enough to give as good as I got. I just wanted to play my cricket and go home in the evening. We had net practice on the right-hand side of the square at The Oval; my job was to bowl, and bowl, and bowl. I fancied myself as a bit of a batter but I wasn't to see a bat for the first two weeks of my professional life. We would bowl three times a day for at least 30 minutes at a time, often a bit more if the senior players fancied batting longer in the afternoon. Most evenings I went home completely drained and getting up the next morning to go and do exactly the same thing began to feel like hard work.

The senior players were an interesting mix of people. Surrey was an underachieving team back then, one trophy in 1982 being the sole success since the last Championship win in 1971. It was to be another 10 years before the next trophy. There was some real talent in our dressing room. Players like Alan Butcher, Jack Richards, Pat Pocock, Monte Lynch and the late Sylvester Clarke, really should have won more silverware during their time at Surrey, but an underachieving side we would remain.

After the first week of pre-season where we had been worked harder than at any time in my life, we left for Spain. No, not for a holiday, but to La Manga, a purpose built sporting complex often used by sports teams and a business interest of our then captain, Pat Pocock. We were allocated villas and I was to share a room with Jonny Robinson and Graham Brown, the other new boys on the staff. We would do plenty of training and cricket practice that week. One training exercise involved a five-mile run around the complex. A few of the lads were under the impression it was one lap around the designated route. However, David Ward seeing the finish line for the first time put in a great sprint finish. The sight of him having to set off for another lap caused a certain amount of hilarity. My fitness at this stage was pretty hopeless; I had never really done any form of training, so this was all pretty new, and painful, to me. I finished third last out of a professional staff of 24 players. The only players who finished behind me were Sylvester Clarke and Alan Butcher, who had a calf strain. This would be the last time I ever struggled in pre-season; I knew I had a lot of work to do.

Cricketing-wise I was coping pretty well. I was enjoying bowling at all these great players. Alec Stewart really stood out for me, a fine player in the making and a good professional, someone you could really learn from. Alec would look after me too. Many times he would talk to me and tell me just to concentrate on my cricket and ignore all the backbiting and jealousy that was rife amongst the senior players. Sylvester Clarke was another who was really exceptional. Sylvester was a big lumbering West Indian, who used to terrify players all around the country. Off a short run-up and often in trainers, Sylvester would unleash 90mph thunderbolts. That was during the day. In the evenings he would drink copious amounts of rum and coke. An athlete he wasn't, but a great man he was. It was a very sad day when we learned of his death from a heart attack in 1999. There were others I didn't feel comfortable around, Jack Richards for one. An immensely talented cricketer, who made the most of his ability and went on to play for England, Jack was the sort of bloke who could make you feel very uncomfortable and I never really enjoyed his company. There was a bit of a 'them and us' attitude, not helped by the fact that even when we were playing in the same team we changed in different dressing rooms. The young lads always felt like second-class citizens and were treated as such, fetching and carrying, cleaning boots, etc. Graham Brown, Jack's understudy, found life incredibly difficult. Jack would order him around, make him whiten his pads and generally be at his beck and call. I can only imagine that is what Jack had to do when he first came on the staff and obviously he thought what he went through was good enough for Brown.

Back home the season started. The first team was fairly established at this stage and I was looking forward to playing a few games for the second team. I had done so the previous year, so was fairly comfortable playing at that level. I didn't have a great start to the season though; I bowled OK without pulling up too many trees. The first team was struggling. There were a couple of injuries and some poor form. There was a sense that the management wanted to make some changes.

I had already been twelfth man for the first team so I had been close. Being twelfth man meant you were a general dogsbody – fetching and carrying, drinks for the bowlers, drinks for the batsmen, it wasn't a lot of fun. I was even twelfth man for Notts when they came to The Oval for the first game of the season. Having to field for the opposition against your own team is a bizarre experience to say the least. Do you make an extra special effort to take a catch? Or do you let a ball through your legs? For a 17-year-old there were too many questions I didn't know the answer to. Fortunately that practice has gone out of the game now.

A game at The Oval against Glamorgan at the start of June was to be my last second-team game for a while. In the second innings of that game

# BICKERS

I took five wickets and that seemed to convince Mickey Stewart that I was ready to make the step up. Not that I was convinced myself. True, I had bowled well in the second team, but the next step up seemed huge. I had only been on the staff for two months and was still so young.

But I got my chance. On Saturday 7th June, Surrey v Derbyshire at The Oval, another dream is realised and I am walking out with the Surrey first team for my debut. Fear and nerves have pretty much taken over at this stage and I am doing my best to hold it all in. Sylvester Clarke bowls the first ball to Kim Barnett and all I can see is Jack Richards diving full length down the leg side to take an incredible catch. 0-1 and I didn't even see the ball!

I came on to bowl after an hour's play. "Don't make a fool of yourself" is my overriding preoccupation at this stage, but fortunately I start well and I bowl two maidens. This is a great settler for a young bowler and soon I am bowling well. I am going past the edge of the bat with trademark away swinging deliveries, but no wicket in my first spell. However, everyone seems happy with what I have done so far. Darren is there watching and over the lunch break I tell him how unlucky I have been. The afternoon session starts and I get another chance, this time with more success. Chris Marples becomes my first wicket, caught behind by Jack Richards. Fair enough it's not Viv Richards as I had dreamt growing up, but Marples, a little known Derbyshire wicket-keeper. It didn't matter really. I got another wicket shortly after and finished with 2-23 after 12 overs. I was ecstatic. We had all bowled well and we had a small lead when it came to our turn to bat. My first ball was from Michael Holding.

Now as a young lad growing up, watching Michael Holding terrorise

# Martin Bicknell

England in 1976 I was expecting the worst and as he ran into bowl I could hardly hear his feet hit the ground. 'Whispering Death' was a perfect nickname for the great man. Fortunately for me I managed to get bat on ball and down the other end where I had my stumps rearranged by Ole Mortensen, the big Danish fast bowler. In the second innings I took another three wickets and we ended up winning the game. I even got a mention in *The Sun* to top it all off.

I had done enough to earn a run in the side. Our next game saw us play Nottinghamshire at Trent Bridge, a game against the great Richard Hadlee, one of my boyhood heroes. There were several great players in that side. Apart from Hadlee they had Clive Rice, Chris Broad, Tim Robinson and Derek Randall. They were a formidable side backed up by a large home crowd. We lost the toss and bowled first. I found the going a little harder this time and although I took three late wickets to clean up the tail I had gone for 72 off my 18 overs. Nottinghamshire had scored 294 all out, but by the close of play we were a Hadlee-inspired three down for not very many. Next day the game was all over. We were bowled out for the second time just after tea on the second day, with Hadlee taking 10 wickets in the match. On a pitch I had struggled to bowl on, he had destroyed the Surrey line-up twice. I had come out to bat in the morning session. We were in all sorts of trouble. For some reason I was batting nine and it felt like two positions too high. Alec Stewart was batting the other end and I was to face Richard Hadlee in top gear. Great. The first ball was back of a length and seamed away and I missed it by miles. The second ball was a little wider, but this time it cut back in and nearly cleaned me up, so to speak. The third, again back of a length, bounced a little more. When I say bounced I mean headed straight for my throat. I threw up my hands, it hit my gloves and lobbed up to Paul Johnson at short leg. Out to the great Richard Hadlee. "Fair enough" I thought, "he's a bit better than me". Unbeknown to me, as I was walking off Hadlee turned to Alec Stewart and said "Three balls is enough for a schoolboy." Well I guess at least he knew who I was even if I had left school a while back.

For that trip to Nottingham I shared a room with Graham Monkhouse. Monkhouse had come to Surrey from Cumbria and had done well for Surrey, but for this game he was twelfth man. It didn't really seem to bother him though. Nottingham, apparently with a ratio of one male to every three females, was the perfect place not to be playing. In the four nights we stayed at the hotel his bed was untouched. I may as well have had a single room to myself. There seemed to be a real drinking and partying culture in the team. Monte Lynch seemed to have a woman for every night of the week, all over the country. And Andy Needham seemed to spend most of the time asleep under a table during match days. After the day's play there would be a card school. Being the gambling type I got involved. My salary of £100 a week wasn't really enough to keep up with the big boys, so invariably I had to leave the game early. Life at Surrey was certainly more interesting than being at school.

My batting at this stage had gone violently downhill. I joined the staff on the back of lots of runs at youth level and had visions of being an all rounder. What I hadn't taken into account was the pace at which the guys at first-team level could bowl. I was very ill-equipped to deal with it, lost my confidence and struggled badly. In my first year on the staff I faced Holding, Marshall, Daniel, Hadlee, Imran Khan and Courtney Walsh. It was no great surprise this set me back a bit.

I was still very green behind the ears. When it came to girls I had no idea what I was doing really. I'd had girlfriends at school but now I was 17 and still hadn't really got to do what most 17-year-olds were doing. After a Nat West Trophy tie in Cheshire the second team were in need of a twelfth man. They were playing at Elland, near Leeds. I volunteered for some reason. I think I was so in love with the game that I preferred to be near a cricket ground rather than go home, and I was always keen to please people. I arrived in the evening and found several members of the team in the bar. It wasn't long before I had had a couple of drinks and with the idea of not playing tomorrow at the forefront of my mind, embarked on a little tour of the local drinking establishments. Flanked by a couple of senior members of the side we ended up in this nightclub, a rather seedy joint, but exactly what we were looking for. I remember sitting on a bar stool minding my own business when a fight broke out next to me and before I knew it I was on the floor. The next thing I know, I am being helped to my feet by a young lady. Egged on by my mates we got talking and ended up going back to the hotel where we were staying for more drinks. My room-mate for the trip was David Thomas, the left-arm quick bowler, who was coming to the end of his career and was also out late drinking. He decided that it would be OK if the girl stayed the night in our room. I was so pissed at this stage I had no idea I was going to lose my virginity and it was all over so quickly I don't think my room-mate even noticed. So that was that. I had finally broken my duck. Word got out pretty quickly and I was the subject of immense piss-taking throughout the next day and for the next few weeks. I was so hung over I could barely keep my eyes open. Fortunately I wasn't called upon to do too much and I was glad to get home that night.

I kept my place in the team and grew in confidence daily. I was receiving good reviews all the time and then I found myself selected for the England Under 19 team. This meant leaving Surrey for the middle part of the season and playing a couple of Test matches against Sri Lanka. I enjoyed being part of a young talented team; Atherton, Hussain and Ramprakash were in the team at the time. However my success came at quite a price when I was struck down by a nasty side strain that caused me to miss six weeks of the season. According to the physio it was caused by overbowling, a result of my spindly frame not being able to cope with the workload I was under. The next winter would see the end of my lightweight appearance. Geoff Arnold took note of what had happened to me and decided I needed to spend a winter with a man called Tim Laskey who turned out to be one of the most eccentric men I have ever met. Over the next 10 winters I would spend many days with Tim, running up sands hills, lifting weights and with him pushing me to my absolute limit. He loved it, and looking back I loved it too. It gave me a great work ethic, something often missing in today's cricketers. One Christmas Eve I took my brother and a couple of mates to try these hills that I was always talking about. The training involved running up the hill – about 40 seconds of running – and then walking down and doing it again. Well, they managed three before two of them threw up and the other one looked like he was going to need hospital attention. They didn't come again. One winter we got up to 12 repetitions of these hills and I felt like I was the fittest man on earth. We would run in all kinds of weather and invariably I would leave training feeling like death warmed up. One of Tim's famous sayings was that it was only physical pain, not mental pain, and you can always deal with the former. He's probably right and having experienced the pain of divorce recently I wouldn't wish that on my worst enemy.

The back end of the 1986 season saw us just miss a Lord's final, losing to Lancashire in the semi at a packed Oval. In the quarter-final we had played Notts and Richard Hadlee bowled superbly, taking 5-17 off 12 overs. It was a master class of seam bowling, I could only sit back and admire. Our score of 204 in 60 overs was way below par. However in our side we had one of the greatest in Sylvester Clarke. Clarke tore into Notts and got us going. We all bowled exceptionally well and won the game by 46 runs. Hadlee scored 55 in a losing cause; I bowled really well at him and loved the challenge of competing against one of the world's best.

The semi-final was a huge affair. It was the first time I had played in a televised match. It only added to the occasion. I made sure I told my Mum to tape the game – I was desperate to see myself on TV. There must have been 10,000 people in the ground and the focal point of the game would be Sylvester Clarke against Clive Lloyd. Clarke and Lloyd didn't get on very well. Clarke was banned from playing for the West Indies after throwing a brick into the crowd in India. As a result of his ban Clarke joined the rebel tour of South Africa. He effectively turned his back on the West Indies. The Inter-Island rivalry was pretty fierce as well with Clarke coming from Barbados and Lloyd from Guyana. We bowled first and early wickets brought Lloyd to the crease. Clarke, on a very fast Oval pitch was terrifyingly quick, but still Lloyd didn't wear a helmet. Clarke beat him five balls in a row with balls that flew past his chin, but he never flinched. He went on to score 65 to get Lancashire up to 229. It was a great innings, full of bravery and courage.

It was a game we should have won easily. Lancashire weren't particularly strong but we froze and got ourselves in a mess chasing the runs. It was only the brilliance of Trevor Jesty that got us anywhere near close as wickets fell all around him. I batted 11, behind Pat Pocock of all people. By this stage of the season my confidence was so low I didn't know which end of the bat to hold. We still needed over 20 runs to win and it was my job, as a 17-year-old, to help win us the game. We edged nearer, more by luck than judgement and got it down to single figures. Finally it came down to just one hit. With only five runs to win, Jesty, who had scored a magnificent century, picked out Graeme Fowler on the deep square leg boundary. It was all over. I had come so close to appearing in a Lord's final at the age of 17, but it was not to be, and the Lancashire players celebrated as the crowd ran on. Jesty was inconsolable, and I just couldn't take it all in. It was the start of a run of losing semi-finals that would label us the great underachievers. After the game for the first time I saw grown men in tears over a cricket match. For some, the thought of never playing in a Lord's final was too much to bear. We won the last Championship game of the season to finish fifth in the table. The prize money for that and getting to the semi-final of the Nat West bought me my first car, as I had just passed my test. A beautiful brown Ford Escort, at a cost of £600, was all mine!

It was the end of my first season in the game – one that had brought me great success. I took 27 wickets at 22 apiece to finish in the Top 10 in the national bowling averages. Batting, I averaged 2.62 which was not so good. I had earned myself a trip to Sri Lanka with England Under 19s. It was all change at The Oval. Pat Pocock retired. Mickey Stewart went off to manage England and a few players were released. In came Darren, Graham Thorpe and David Smith from Worcestershire and a few younger lads from my Surrey Under 19 days. The biggest arrival was Ian Greig as captain. Ian, younger brother of Tony, had plied his trade at Sussex before a knee injury forced him out of the game. Geoff Arnold, who had taken over first-team affairs from Mickey, was seeking more of a disciplinarian as leader. Geoff heard that Ian Greig was seeking a move back into the game and thought he would be an ideal man for the job.

# Early Years

At the start of the 1987 season I had just returned from a very successful trip to Sri Lanka and I thought life would all be roses. I felt I had really come of age as a cricketer on that tour. I had such control with my bowling and even scored a 50 in one Test match. As a result I approached the season with great expectation. But after the previous season where I could do no wrong, all of a sudden life wasn't so easy. I struggled with injury, a loss of form and loss of confidence. My stats in 1987 look quite good, but in truth I didn't bowl that well and at times found Ian Greig very hard to get on with. Added to that, the atmosphere in the team hadn't really improved. My form was so bad that on one occasion I ended up in tears after a spell at The Oval against Kent where I couldn't even land the ball in the other half of the wicket.

Looking back at it now, it had all happened so early. I had basically left school and gone straight into the first team and had immediate success. Now for the come down. A young player will often have a good first year and then regress in the second. It happened to Graham Thorpe after me. I was too young and fragile to deal with it. I was mentally soft and I wasn't physically strong enough either. The game at Northants in the second round of the Nat West Trophy saw me open the bowling with Sylvester Clarke. He, of course, bowled with the wind, which meant I had to bowl into it. After one over I proved to the captain I couldn't do it. The wind was too strong and I had to wait until Clarke finished his spell the other end. This didn't impress the other bowlers in the team who had to come and do the job I was supposed to do. To top it off, we lost the game and were dumped out of the competition. It wasn't all bad of course; I took my first five-wicket haul later in the season against Somerset, including that of Steve Waugh, a man I would run into at a later date. But on the whole I was way too inconsistent for my liking.

One of the highlights of the season came at Edgbaston in a game against Warwickshire, when, due to one of our openers falling ill at the last moment, Darren got the call to make his first-class debut. He made 60 odd and I confess I was probably more nervous than he was. I was always nervous watching him bat in those days – though that disappeared when we had to play against each other later in our careers.

The low point of the season came in another semi-final defeat – this time at the hands of Yorkshire in front of a partisan crowd at Headingley. The Yorkshire crowd didn't like Sylvester Clarke too much. Whether it was the colour of his skin or the fact that he hated Yorkshire batsmen I don't know. In a previous game Clarke had destroyed the Yorkshire batting at The Oval, his hostility and pace proving too much for the 'gun shy' Yorkshire batters. He took abuse from the crowd throughout the game, most of it very unpleasant. I took my fair share too. Being 18 I didn't have a clue how to react and just gave it back. They had me for breakfast. I concentrated on my cricket from then on. I bowled well, 3-29 off 11 overs, but with Jim Love, the burly Yorkie, smashing David Thomas for three huge sixes onto the Rugby stand, Yorkshire scored too many at the end of the innings. We lost by 76 runs and it was two semis played, two defeats.

That winter I took myself off to New Zealand to play for a club side called Suburbs New Lynn in Auckland. I had been to Australia with Surrey Under 18s a couple of years prior to this trip, but now I was on my own. The flight took 36 hours, and as I got to the airport late I was stuck at the back of the plane between two chain smokers. I landed in Auckland and knew no one. I had left my family and Emma, my girlfriend, and I was taking a journey into the unknown. I was picked up by one of the club officials who drove me to where I was staying. I dropped off my luggage and went straight to the ground to practise. I was 18 years old and it felt like they were expecting Richard Hadlee to turn up. As an overseas professional you are expected to take loads of wickets and score match winning runs. The first couple of games showed I was no Richard Hadlee. The cricket was harder than I thought. An opening batsman we played against took me for 40 off my first four overs. I wanted to pack up and go home. Things did improve a bit and I took five wickets in one game to win the match, but value for money I was not.

The idea of these trips away in the winter was for a young cricketer to get experience of playing in foreign conditions. You could work on your game, get away from your parents and come back a more rounded player. Well, it didn't quite work out like that. Being in a foreign country without too many friends can be very difficult. It was also my first experience of living on my own. I had no idea about cooking; I ended up microwaving sausages for dinner. And I certainly knew nothing about operating washing machines and cleaning. The club got me a job in a factory, cutting out plastic shapes; I lasted three days doing that. I have done some crap jobs in my time but this was definitely the worst. Fortunately the club then said I could basically do nothing and get paid, which seemed like a much better idea, so I ended up playing a lot of golf and drinking too much. Cricket wasn't nearly as important as it should have been. I did like New Zealand though and made some great friends. One day one of the guys took me out horse riding. I had never been near a horse before, and they certainly don't come with a set of instructions. We rode for four hours; the horses were cantering and galloping, up and down hills. I hung on for dear life. I couldn't walk for a week. I also spent two weeks on a yacht over Christmas and New Year, sailing around the top end of the North Island. I spent the first few days throwing up and on the way back into Auckland we hit quite a storm. I ended up at the front of the yacht doing my Titanic impression. It was all good fun.

There was better news on the horizon though, as I was selected to go to Australia for the Youth World Cup in February. I would be playing against Brian Lara, Inzamam ul Haq, Stuart Law and Sanath Jayasuria, to name a few. My back was still giving me a bit of a problem; don't think the horse riding really helped. I was sure I would be fine once I got to Australia though.

On my last night in New Zealand the team threw a bit of a party for me. I knew they had something special lined up, so to be clever I thought I would make a run for it. This, after I had already thrown up, was not a good move. I bolted down the stairs in the clubhouse forgetting that after a skin-full my co-ordination wouldn't be the greatest. I missed the last step on the stairs and landed very badly on my ankle. Even allowing for the fact that I was so hammered, I thought I had broken my ankle. I couldn't walk and I lived a good three miles from the club. I had a problem: stay and risk alcohol poisoning, or drive home and risk being arrested and thrown out of the country. I drove. I have never concentrated more in my life and just about got home in one piece. Next day I had to fly to Australia and meet up with my brother before joining up with the England Under 19 squad in Melbourne. Already suffering with a suspect back I now had an ankle the size of a football. It wasn't shaping up well for the World Cup.

I spent a good couple of days with my brother. He too was playing league cricket. My ankle problem subsided and we practised together at his club side. The Aussies in his side were full of it as per normal, giving the English stick whenever they could. You either sink or swim in that country. You can't afford to be mentally soft in the presence of Aussies. It's no surprise they are such a strong sporting nation. They live and breathe sport. The weak fall away and the strong dominate. As a team, the England Under 19 team would find that out soon enough.

The World Cup tournament started and we progressed well, beating India, West Indies, Pakistan and Zimbabwe, but losing to Australia and Sri Lanka. During the tournament I hadn't been at my best. I wasn't very fit and was struggling for rhythm. The coach on that trip was Bob Cottam, who went on to coach England's bowlers. We didn't see eye to eye about my bowling and I didn't really feel he could help me. I needed Geoff Arnold to have a look at my action, not someone who hardly knew me. Bob famously said on that trip that he thought Peter Martin was a club 3rd XI bowler; Martin went on to play for England in eight Tests and 20 one-day internationals.

We got to the semi-finals but ran into the Aussies again and got smashed out of sight. I missed the game through a back injury again and to be honest I couldn't wait to get home. It had been a long winter away from home and I didn't enjoy it. I was injured, unfit and my performances weren't up to scratch.

Back in England 1988 wasn't a whole lot better. I took 50 first-class wickets for the first time, but I found myself in and out of the side far too regularly for my liking. I just wasn't consistent enough in my or Ian Greig's terms. I was still quite emotionally fragile and found it very difficult to cope with the pressures of playing sport for a living. It was also hard dealing with a group of guys who were far more mature than I was. I didn't always get the support I needed either; Geoff Arnold was very much a 'get on with it' type of coach and didn't really understand my lack of confidence. Ian Greig was just a hard South African without a hint of compassion in him. I needed to become much harder as a person if I was to really make my mark at this level. I was far too soft for the world of professional sport.

There were some high points though. We played Cambridge University at The Oval in mid-June and as I had been in and out of the team it would be a good opportunity to get some overs under my belt. In the first innings I bowled OK, but on a flat Oval wicket I didn't really look like taking a wicket. I finished with 0-42 off 16 overs. It was disappointing. I was expected to take a hatful of wickets. Something wasn't right. I spent a bit of time with Geoff Arnold before the last morning of the game. He spotted something in my action and I was able to correct it. Cue second innings and I became a different bowler. After Tony Gray took the first wicket I took the next nine. I finished with 9-45 and a career best. It just goes to show you the value of a good coach, and Arnold was the best. I bowled well and it was just one of those days where everything goes your way. It should have kick-started my season. I didn't even get into the side for the next game. It was one hell of a frustrating year.

Team-wise we were making progress. We finished fourth in the Championship and got to the semi-finals of the Nat West Trophy before being soundly beaten by Middlesex. The highlight of the game for us was Alec Stewart's unbeaten hundred as we failed to chase 258. Alec was really coming of age as a cricketer now and this innings showed he could perform on the big stage. Nevertheless, it was another semi-final defeat. We were getting closer as a team but there was still something missing. How to win was something we didn't know. We would get ourselves into positions of strength and then we wouldn't be able to get over the winning line.

At the end of 1988 we all needed a change. We needed a fresh start. Clarke, Richards, Smith, Butcher and Jesty had all gone, to be replaced by younger faces. We signed Dirk Tazelaar from Queensland as our overseas player and players like David Ward, Paul Atkins and Tony Murphy came to the club. For all Greig's faults he wasn't afraid to confront a problem – the problem at the time being the senior players. He got rid of what he thought the problems were and gave youth its chance to shine. Personally, the winter of 1988/9 was the pivotal moment in my development; I had played at being a professional cricketer and had mixed results. I knew I had talent, I was never going to be a quick bowler but I had good control and could swing the ball both ways. All I had to do was train harder and become more consistent with the ball in my hand. I could also do with growing up a bit and developing a stronger mentality.

So, it was back to Tim Laskey and the dreaded sand hills. This time it was different though. I had a desire to succeed and Tim was the ideal man to help me. We did quite a bit of work that winter on building up my confidence, how to cope with pressure situations and just basically toughening up. We sat in his kitchen for hours and I poured out all my feelings about cricket. I had no real confidence with the new ball in my hand. It should be the best time to bowl but I approached it with fear. I would much rather bowl with an older ball when the pressure was off a bit. With the new ball I felt an expectation to succeed, and that continually got the better of me. That winter we developed a strategy for dealing with pressure situations. If ever I was feeling really nervous I could take out the piece of paper we worked on, reinforce the positive and take away the negative feelings. It would stand me in good stead for the rest of my career.

But Tim was still slightly mad in my eyes. Just for laughs and because he could, on his 50th birthday he lined himself up a special treat. He was going to run one hill for every year of his age. Yes that's right, 50 hills – no matter how long it took him. (Bear in mind that 12 hills is the most I have ever run, at my very fittest.) He succeeded too. It took him forever to complete, but he did it all the same. I have an enormous amount of respect for Tim and I will always be grateful for the work he put in with me.

During the winter I was back playing football. Darren and I and the three Thorpe brothers would represent Old Farnhamians at Farnham College. I was no Farnhamian but the football was great. Saturday afternoons generally meant no training with Tim – a good thing. However, there was still a chance the big slow lumbering centre-half would kick lumps out of you. I played centre-forward and had a pretty good goals to game ratio. Graham Thorpe was a very good player having represented England Under 15s. Darren was still in goal, too slow to play anywhere else! And Thorpey's Dad was manager. We played some teams who weren't great but would delight in having a fight. The Thorpe brothers would take it in turns to get sent off, and Thorpe senior would swear for the entire 90 minutes. "A goal a game at the far post" was his favourite saying, as I generally failed to be in the right position at the right time. It was great fun; however, the more we got recognised the more vulnerable we were to serious injury. In one game – I think it was Wonersh away, (admittedly not Man U v Liverpool but a big local derby all the same) – we ran rings around them and I scored a hat-trick. During the second half, the centre-half was becoming more and more irate by the minute. After I scored my third goal he turned to me and said "if you score another effing goal I am going to break your effing legs". Nice. My football career stopped shortly afterwards. However it was perfect for the long winter months. And it kept us in good shape.

In those days the cricket side would report back on 1st April, do two weeks of intense physical training and combine that with net practice and warm-up matches. Competitive cricket would start around the third week in April. Nowadays things are a lot different. Most counties will pay their players for at least seven months, meaning they all report back as a squad on 1st March. This gives the squad more time for training in the first month before cricket starts at the beginning of April. For too long cricket has lagged behind with its approach to fitness. When I first started playing, back in 1986, players would turn up on 1st April having done virtually no training whatsoever and expect to get fit over the first two weeks of pre-season in order to play cricket for the next six months. It just wasn't professional enough, and although cricket has made huge strides over the last 20 years to catch up, we still lag behind most sports when it comes to an attitude towards fitness in general. I was lucky in the fact that very early in my career I got to see what it was like being fit and unfit at the start of a season and the effect it had on my performance.

I hit the 1989 season in great shape and with new found confidence. I had put so much into my off-season. I was at the front of all the fitness tests, bowling well in the nets and couldn't wait for the season to start. It felt like a new beginning. Old faces had gone and the team had a fresh look to it. Only Graham Clinton and Ian Greig were over 30.

Early on in the season we were at Lord's playing Middlesex on a typical flat Lord's wicket. Middlesex were 'the team' of this period. Players like Gatting, Downton, Emburey, Fraser and Tufnell were all established England players and it would be a great test for me. We lost the game but in the process I bowled a staggering 63 overs in the match and took eight wickets for 167 runs. All the work I had put in that winter had really paid off. My fitness and my form meant I was able to compete with these great players and now I felt I could really kick on and push for higher honours.

As a team we were still short of many things and the prospect of silverware still seemed a million miles away. We finished twelfth out of 17 teams that year. Our overseas player, Dirk Tazelaar, had left early that season with a back injury and we only ended up winning four games all year, a poor return from 22 games played. The Benson and Hedges was a shambles, with us finishing bottom of our group and losing to the Combined Universities after failing to chase down just 116. We lost in the quarter-finals of the Nat West Trophy to Hampshire. The Sunday League was a little more encouraging; a sixth-place finish at least showed we might have some potential here. Surrey fans may well remember a game at Northampton that year when, decimated by injuries, we were so short of bowlers that Geoff Arnold, our then coach, had to play and open the bowling. Aged 44, Arnold bowled six overs and took 1-7 before a shoulder injury stopped him in his tracks. It was an incredible performance for someone who hadn't played any cricket for over five years. If we were going to win anything as a team we had to make massive improvements. The team contained too many people just not good enough to wear the Surrey shirt. Additionally we had a collection of inexperienced cricketers and a captain who now couldn't bowl because of a knee injury. We had no overseas player or match winner. Both Tony Murphy and I took 65 wickets that year but that wasn't enough to win trophies. We had to get in a 100-wicket a year man.

My opening bowling partner in the 1989 season was the aforementioned Tony Murphy. Murph had come down after leaving Lancashire and immediately made his mark in and around the team. He wasn't what you would describe a natural athlete. A portly, barrel-chested lad, he would run through brick walls for you but would probably be unable to complete a decathlon. On one pre-season training trip we went to Lanzarote for a week's training and bonding. It was a popular hangout for Olympic athletes such as Linford Christie and the German sprinting team. As you can imagine back in 1989 professional cricket had still to grasp the idea that you needed to be fit to play cricket, so our collection of under-prepared cricketers did not look overly good compared to these finely tuned athletes. Our physio at the time, a man called John Deary, ex-army man and top bloke, had us in the middle of the running track playing what can only be described as kids' party games. It was highly embarrassing. However, this was not where the embarrassment stopped. As part of our running training we were now to join the Olympic athletes on the track as we did our 400 metre runs. Murph, a typical Lancastrian, looked a picture. Dressed in what can only be described as the worst pair of beach shorts imaginable, a singlet and 10-year-old trainers, Murph was running alongside Linford Christie! What on earth the German athletes made of it who knows? Cricket had a lot to learn. It wasn't the only slightly embarrassing thing to happen that week either. One night towards the end of the trip we thought we would let our hair down a little bit and we discovered Karaoke night in the resort's main bar. Mark Butcher, then a young lad, got up on stage and performed the best Tina Turner impression you will ever see, wig and all. A star was born. The lads had a good night and most went home reasonably early as we had a gym session the next morning. I say most of the lads. It was pretty clear the next morning who hadn't. Waqar didn't show up, Graham Thorpe arrived late, looking fairly horrific and Keith Medlycott spent most of the gym session with a paper bin next to him just in case he was going to throw up. Needless to say Geoff Arnold wasn't overly impressed, especially as we were once again sharing a gym with top class athletes. We never went back to Lanzarote, funnily enough!

Personally, things couldn't have gone any better for me in 1989. I had bowled over 600 overs, taken 65 wickets at 26 apiece, earned my first-team cap and been selected for the England A tour to Zimbabwe and Kenya the following February. The responsibility of being the number one bowler in the team had brought out the best in me. With the Whittingdale sponsorship and England touring money Emma and I bought a flat in Sutton for £65,000. I was getting tired of the long journeys into work, so living closer would help. I could also stop doing all the crappy jobs to earn a little more money. No more DIY shops and driving cars all over England. I was heading for the big time – or so I thought.

England had been smashed by Australia at home and rumours of another rebel tour to South Africa were rife. South Africa at this stage was still not being allowed back into international cricket and the rebel tour was the talk of the cricketing world. Top England players like Mike Gatting, Neil Foster, Graham Dilley and Chris Broad signed up for big money and therefore served three-year bans from international cricket. Some of the players would not play for England again, but financially they were better off. Blood money it was called. The upshot of this tour was that with so many England players leaving the scene there would be opportunities for younger players to force their way into the England team. Devon Malcolm took his opportunity and really made a name for himself on the tour to the West Indies, as did Nasser Hussain and Alec Stewart. The England A tours were a new concept. Keith Fletcher would manage the tour, Mark Nicholas would captain it, and Surrey had a good representation in the squad, with me and Darren being selected along with the up and coming star Graham Thorpe. I had heard so much about how good a coach Keith Fletcher was and couldn't wait to hear what he had to say about the game in general and my game in particular. Ultimately I would be disappointed with what I heard.

# Martin Bicknell

# On the Fringes of England

The summer of 1989 had been my finest yet, I had come of age as a cricketer. Sixty-five wickets at 26 runs per wicket had earned me the 'bowler of the year' award and, better still, a place on the England A Tour to Kenya and Zimbabwe. Darren and Graham Thorpe were also selected, so it had a nice Surrey flavour to it. Mark Nicholas was captain, with Mike Atherton his deputy, and the tour was managed by Keith Fletcher. The main England tour was to the West Indies. Alec Stewart would make his debut on that tour. Keith Medlycott, who had bowled beautifully for Surrey all year, was going as second spinner. Surrey at last had good representation with England.

England had had a torrid time against the Australians in 1989, and with the rebel tour taking half that team this was a great opportunity for the younger players to really stake a claim. For the first time there were organised regional net sessions in the winter, along with some really tough training sessions. I was still training with Tim Laskey and this, along with the England sessions, got me into great shape. Geoff Boycott was employed by England for the first time and he gave the batters a bit of a fright by insisting that the net bowlers bowl off 18 yards to recreate the pace of bowling they were likely to face in the Caribbean. We heard all sorts of horror stories about batters getting hit left right and centre during Sir Geoffrey's sessions!

We left for Kenya at the start of February. Being part of an England setup was what I had always dreamed of and I couldn't wait to get started. Having landed in Nairobi we checked in at our accommodation and then set out for a bit of light training to get over the flight. I immediately got off on the wrong foot with Fletcher by turning up with the wrong training kit. I blamed jet lag.

We trained hard. It was ridiculously hot and we all suffered. Coming out of a cold English winter into the height of a Kenyan summer was a bit of an issue and one that would nearly have a tragic ending. Our first game of the tour was against a local team and I got a game, but I suffered from stage fright and my first few overs went for plenty. I came back pretty well and we ended up winning the game. The next match I was left out as part of the early rotation policy and we lost. During the break between the second and third games most of the team went down with food poisoning. I was sharing a room with Darren at the time and he spent most of the day in the bathroom throwing up. With severe trouble the other end as well he made a wonderful room-mate.

During one of the practice days we noticed Steve Rhodes had a problem. A naturally fit lad 'Bumpy' looked so ill we thought he was going down with something. The physio thought there was a real issue so they rushed him off to hospital, and word came back that he was in serious trouble. He had trained so hard that with the dehydration and illness that was going around he had put himself in real danger of not pulling through.

Naturally the team were worried sick. When he eventually did, the relief was incredible. After a short rest in hospital 'Bumpy' was able to rejoin the tour. Our last match was cancelled due to the fact that we only had seven fit players. It was so disappointing, I was just itching to play as I so wanted to make up for my horror start in the first match.

After our short stay in Kenya we moved on to Zimbabwe. It was almost a relief to get out of Kenya after all the trouble we had encountered. And when a steak sandwich appeared on the room service menu it was like a whole new world had opened up.

Chris Lewis had left our tour to go to the West Indies. An incredibly talented cricketer, Chris was seen as the great hope of English cricket. Ricardo Ellcock had suffered a back injury at the start of the tour and been forced home, so Chris took his place. I was disappointed it wasn't me, but my time would come. Lewis remained the great enigma of English cricket. Too many problems followed him around. A natural showman, Lewis was so talented that he could play in most teams as either a batter or bowler, but his results do not do justice to his ability. Lewis came to Surrey and played a big part in our early success, but he came with baggage. He was fortunate in a way that Adam Hollioake and David Gilbert had taken over at Surrey and they gave him the bit of leeway he required. Not one for conforming to rules, Lewis would do his own thing, so as part of a winning side you could accommodate him for a while. When he left Surrey after a couple of years it came as no real surprise. You always felt with Chris that he needed to keep moving.

England's tour of the West Indies started in spectacular style with a win against all the odds in Jamaica. Devon Malcolm had inspired England and shocked the West Indies. They weren't used to losing matches at home and especially not to England after the decade of dominance they had enjoyed over us. When we heard the news it gave us a massive boost at the start of our Zimbabwe leg. We all so wanted to be part of the new-look England.

I didn't really impress in Kenya so it wasn't a great surprise to be left out of the first two one-day games against Zimbabwe. I was very disappointed though and desperate to make my mark. We got off to a great start and won both games. So good were our performances that the management kept the same side for the opening 'Test' match, also played in Harare. During the game we met Robert Mugabe. He lived just across the road from the sports club and every time he left or re-entered his house there was the most extraordinary noise of police cars and sirens. We didn't give too much thought to what he was about to do to Zimbabwe at the time. He was just another dignitary we had to meet.

The next leg of our journey would take us to Bulawayo, a sleepy town in the middle of the country. Mark Nicholas, who was captain of the tour, made a special point of keeping me informed about plans as to when I would get my chance. I really appreciated that. It is so easy for a young cricketer to get disillusioned on tour when not playing. I have to say though that I was more impressed by Nicholas as a captain than as a player.

I did get my chance in the second 'Test' coming in for Steve Watkin as we rotated our bowlers. After winning the toss we batted for over two days – Mike Atherton with a hundred and Richard Blakey with a double. We eventually got a bowl just before lunch on the third day. I immediately made an impact by taking the first three wickets as the ball swung for me. After all the waiting around to play it was great to make that sort of impression. Unfortunately we ran into David Houghton who battled away for a double hundred and the game petered out in a draw. My contribution was 4-74 off 32 overs – a really satisfying effort in the conditions. During the game we had a rest day, and were invited to a house with horses, tennis courts and a pool. We thought it would be a great idea to go horse riding. Now I am no horseman and these animals could really shift. Galloping down a dirt path Darren's horse caught sight of a snake and stopped. The horse stopped but Darren didn't and he went straight over the handlebars. All this in the middle of a 'Test' match. He was lucky to come out of it unscathed or else he would have had a job explaining his injury to the management.

The tour ended back at Harare with another draw. We won the series 1-0 after the first 'Test' win and overall we had played the better cricket. Most of the players left the tour with enhanced reputations and the concept of 'A' tours looked to have a good future. I had a very good report and approached the next season at home feeling optimistic. It would be a season that would see my status elevated to that of full England player. The arrival of Waqar Younis at Surrey helped me immensely. I took loads of wickets off the back of his bowling and learnt the art of reverse swing. At the end of the season I had pipped Phil Defreitas for the last bowling spot to go to Australia. It was a dream come true. Of all the tours to get on this was the one. Four months touring Australia and New Zealand would be top of my list of things to do in a lifetime, and I was getting paid for it. Add in the fact I would get to see the Ashes close up, and I was so excited I could barely keep my feet on the ground.

Getting on the tour was one thing but the financial side of it was even better. I would get £20,000 for the tour – this along with the fact I was still being paid by Patrick Whittingdale not to join any rebel tour in the future. Patrick Whittingdale was a wealthy cricket lover who got involved in cricket after the rebel tour threatened to rob England of all its players. His idea was to pick two young cricketers, me and Nasser Hussain, and pay us our summer salary in the winter to stop us joining another rebel tour. Now, I had no intention of joining any rebel tour but this contract, over three years, was too good to be true. I was earning £15,000 a year at Surrey, doubled by Whittingdale and now I had another £20,000 to add to that. It may not seem like a lot of money now, but back then I thought all my Christmases had come at once.

I have to admit I was very much in awe of all the players around me at the start of the Australia tour. Gooch, Gower, Lamb, Larkins and Small were all big names and to be honest I felt a little bit lost. But the younger brigade of Stewart, Tufnell, Fraser and Atherton I knew better.

The tour started in Perth. I was immediately struck by all the attention we received and to be honest I loved it. We had free food, drinks, sun glasses and even trainers. I could get used to this, I thought. I made the first team in the traditional opener at Lilac Hill. It was supposed to be a gentle start to the tour, a chance for the batters to get an innings under their belt and the bowlers to bowl some overs. The Aussies didn't see it quite like that. They saw it as an opportunity to get one over the 'Poms' early on, to undermine any confidence we may have had. Dennis Lillee was playing for the opposition at the age of 41 and still looked as if he could be playing Test cricket. A few of the Western Australia players turned out as well. It was no 'friendly'. I struggled early on, nerves getting the better of me, but we won. Stewart got 70 not out on his return to his old club. For the next game we moved on to the WACA ground for a day nighter against a Western Australia Select XI. This time I made my mark – three early wickets and a bit of aggression made me headline news the next day. I was pretty fired up and exchanged words with a few of the Aussie batters. We lost the game but with the ball swinging and the hard bouncy pitch really suiting my bowling, I had convinced everyone I could play a part on this tour. Back then the England touring teams always took on a young bowler, more for experience than to play a major part in the tour. It didn't bother me though. I was in Australia and loving it.

I missed the first four-day game of the tour in Perth before we moved on to Adelaide to play South Australia. Adelaide has a big reputation as a bowler's nightmare and so it proved for me. After the initial promise I had shown in Western Australia things went pear-shaped pretty quickly. My first spell went everywhere as I struggled to make any impression. I did eventually end up with three wickets but they were expensive. The honeymoon period was over. It was going to be tough on these pitches. I took another two wickets in the second innings but we lost. I felt a bit out of my depth. The step up was going to be bigger than I thought. By this stage Graham Gooch was having a real problem with a hand injury he picked up in Perth and Allan Lamb had taken over the captaincy. I overheard a conversation he was having with another player about me during the game. It went along the lines of me not having the pace to trouble the best players and I wasn't really up to it. Not exactly what you want to hear from the captain.

The first Test in Brisbane came around pretty quickly. I was never really in the hunt to make my debut, even though Jon Agnew in his column for the *Today* newspaper thought I might be a good option with the ball likely to swing. I was more than happy just to sit and watch. The atmosphere was unbelievable and as 'fielding twelfth man' I got out on the pitch quite a lot in the game and loved it. We were bowled out for 190 in the first innings before bowling Australia out for 150, giving us a lead of 40. However Terry Alderman, revelling in the swinging conditions, took six wickets to rout England for just 114 and the Test was over within three days. It was a draining experience. All the pre-Test hype about winning back the Ashes had gone straight out of the window. 1-0 down in Australia seems like a mountain to climb to win the series, and so it proved.

In those days the squad for the tour was the squad for the one-day internationals. There was no separate squad as we have now. Normally, I probably wouldn't have made the one-day team but it was going to be a chance for me to play a few games. There was a whole month between Test matches and that would be filled with endless flights all over Australia playing in a tri-series one-day competition with New Zealand. We started with New Zealand at Perth and I was in the side, nervous as hell, my first proper international. I got off to a great start removing John Wright, and with the ball swinging and bouncing bowled well to take 2-36 off my 10 overs. We ran out easy winners.

We stayed in Perth for the big Sunday game against Australia. Emma, my girlfriend at the time had come out to join the tour for a while. When she arrived things just weren't right between us and I found myself in a very awkward situation. I spent the night on the phone to my Mum, wandering around the foyer of the hotel, anything to stay out of our room.

I hardly slept at all. It was scarcely the best preparation for the big game. Next day we got hammered. I did hit 31 not out off 25 balls at the end of our innings, but bowled pretty poorly despite getting Border and Mark Waugh off successive deliveries.

My relationship with Emma ended with her going back to England soon after that game. It was very hard on her and I didn't handle the situation well at all. It was reported in the papers that I dumped her for an Aussie girl called Rebecca. Rebecca and I would eventually get engaged, but this wasn't the case at the time. We had met, but nothing was going on between us, (whatever Emma still thinks about it). Emma and I put our differences behind us and she very successfully ran both my Benefit and Testimonial Years as my secretary.

After another good game against New Zealand in Sydney we ended up in Brisbane to take on the Aussies again – and in particular Dean Jones. Jones would become my nemesis throughout the rest of the tour. I am convinced he decided to get after me whenever possible just to destroy my confidence. Jones was the sort of Australian you felt even his own team-mates didn't like: brash, arrogant and full of himself. A great player with an impressive record in the game, but a personality that meant you would cross the street to avoid talking to him. In this particular game Jones scored 145 – a brilliant innings, scored off just 136 balls. I didn't quite get the ball in the right place at the end of the innings and most of them went back over my head into the commentary booth. Worse, next up was a four-day game just before Christmas in Ballarat against Jones's state side, Victoria. Once again I bowled and he hit me all over the ground. One shot cleared the pavilion some 100 yards away. If he was looking for some kind of mental disintegration he got it. I was shattered. Confidence that I had built up over the early part of the tour had evaporated and now I didn't know when my next game was going to be.

The second Test was the Boxing Day match at the MCG, the biggest ground I had ever seen. It was full to the rafters. Gooch was back after his nightmare hand injury that had required surgery. The atmosphere in the camp was getting a little frosty though. Gooch and Gower weren't getting on at all. Gower was part of the old school, a cricketer who enjoyed his time away from the game and played in a relaxed manner. At times you could see this really didn't sit well with Gooch or Mickey Stewart who were after a hungrier set of players. They wanted cricketers who would train harder and practice better. I got on with Gower really well on that tour; he came across as a really nice bloke with an encouraging word here and there. But my relationship with Gooch never got out of first gear. Throughout the whole trip he hardly spoke to me. It was as if he didn't know what to say. I was a 20-year-old on the hardest tour of all and I got nothing from him. I know he could be a bit shy. I found him much easier to get on with in 1993, but in Australia I hardly got a sentence out of him.

We lost the Melbourne Test because of an inspired Bruce Reid. On a very slow wicket he took 13 wickets in one of the finest exhibitions of bowling you could ever wish to see. It was such a shame his career was wrecked by injury. Being 6' 8" had its advantages when it came to bowling fast, but a frame like that brought too many injuries with it.

In the Sydney Test another very flat wicket greeted us and we came close to pulling off an unlikely win. This was a game that saw the emergence of Phil Tufnell as a quality Test bowler. Picked as understudy to Eddie Hemmings, Tufnell looked the better bowler for most of the tour. Tuffers did come with a lot of baggage though. Throughout his career he ran into trouble, on and off the field. On the field he could be a genius with the ball in hand, but in the field or batting he made Monty Panesar look like Don Bradman. Tuffers was terrified of the ball. Anything above medium pace would send him diving for all sorts of body protection. Often he was out of the frame altogether whilst getting his stumps rearranged by a nasty fast bowler. In the field he could be pretty hopeless too, and the Aussies had a great time with him. Tuffers was also terrified of flying and would often be seen in the executive lounge of the airport downing a couple of quick drinks before boarding. On one flight down to Geraldton from Perth, the turbulence got so bad we hit our heads on the roof of the plane. Tuffers nearly had a heart attack. For all his problems in and around the game though, he was bloody good value as a tourist.

Tuffers wasn't the only character on the tour. We had Jack Russell who virtually never left his hotel bedroom except to play cricket. He also used to wash his own clothes and hang them around the bedroom. Sharing a room with Jack was certainly an experience – one I first tasted in Perth. I had been out at a restaurant and got back about 10pm. I walked into our room and was confronted with Jack's washing strewn all over the room. It was hanging off lights, on curtain rails and on the television. His theory was that hotel washing machines were going to damage his kit so he didn't want to take that risk. Jack would also have this ritual at lunchtime during matches, of only eating Weetabix with warm milk. As twelfth man it was your responsibility to have this ready for him as he walked off. The milk had to be just the right temperature and the Weetabix soaked for just the right length of time. All the bizarre behaviour aside, Jack and I got on great. He has a passion about his cricket that very few can lay claim to. Our scorer for that trip was a lovely guy called Clem Driver. Clem drank scotch every other day and used to give himself a day off in between. Clem's 'day off' meant he drank wine instead. Sadly Clem passed away a couple of years ago.

After the third Test at Sydney the fringe players got their chance in a couple of state games before the fourth Test at Adelaide. With no Dean Jones to worry me I could settle in and bowl. There was the thought that if I bowled well I would stand a good chance of playing at Adelaide. I did bowl well and towards the end of the second game in Queensland, with a few wickets under my belt, I pushed a bit harder and in that final spell I did what all bowlers dread – I tore the intercostal muscle in my side. On inspection by the physio it was agreed I would have a cortisone injection in my ribs to clear it up quickly. By this time I had missed my chance in the fourth Test and subsequently the fifth in Perth. What I didn't realise at the time was the long-term damage I had done by having the injection. I was trying to get fit for the New Zealand leg of the trip and the three one-day games out there. I desperately wanted to play again so the injection was the best course of action.

The Queensland state game will always be remembered for the Tiger Moth incident. Unbeknown to us, David Gower and John Morris had left the ground during the game with a photographer to have a little plane ride. Sitting there watching the game, we saw a plane coming through the floodlight pylons and something fell out and hit the ground. We didn't really give it much thought at the time until the end of the day. The press were all over the tour manager Peter Lush to find out what was going on.

Gower thought it would be a great idea to drop water bombs in the direction of Allan Lamb. Lush and Mickey Stewart were fuming. What were they thinking of? You would have to ask them. It cost them a large fine and probably ended John Morris's England career. It didn't help the management's relationship with David Gower either.

The Ashes went in Adelaide, although we did get a draw. But the defeat in Perth meant it was 3-0 to the Aussies. A fair result overall. We just weren't good enough. It would be another 14 years and seven attempts before we won back the Ashes. Alec Stewart would play his whole career against the Aussies and not win a series.

On to New Zealand for three one-day games and the relatively relaxed surroundings. I always thought New Zealand was a beautiful country and the people just that bit friendlier than the Aussies. They played their cricket hard though. New Zealand had developed into a fighting team and in their own back yard would take some beating. I proved my fitness in the nets but I knew in my heart there was something not quite right in my side. I was sore but carried on. My bowling suffered and after two games I was left out for the third. At that stage of the tour I was actually hoping not to play, my fragile confidence not being really strong enough for international cricket. I had built up a very good relationship with Rebecca over the second half of the tour and I was really looking forward to going back to Perth to see her. The length of the tours in those days was just huge. We were away for nearly four months and we used 20 players. For all the problems I had – the Dean Jones mauling, the injury and the break up of a long-term relationship – I loved being on tour with England. I loved the attention, the atmosphere and being part of an England team. I did have some success, mixed in with disappointments, but I firmly believe that made me stronger in the long run and hardened me up. It certainly stood me in good stead for the next time I pulled on an England shirt on.

# Back To Surrey

I had really enjoyed the England tour; I loved the attention and the glamour of it all. I had had a taste of it and I wanted more. The end of the tour was great too. I took a month off and spent it in Perth with Rebecca. Perth is a fantastic place for a holiday. It might be verging on the dull side to live there permanently but for a holiday I can't think of many better places. Of course I was still very much in the limelight in and around Perth. The nation is sports mad and they really know their players. I had some success in between the occasional nightmare on tour and the Aussies respected the fact that I gave it a good crack. They love their sportsmen to be competitive and up for a fight and I was certainly in that category.

I had a lot of things to sort out when I got home. Rebecca would come over in the summer to live with me in the flat I had previously shared with Emma. I knew I would get a pretty frosty reception from Emma on my return; we hadn't really spoken since she left Australia and I expected the worst. To be fair to her she didn't have that big an axe to grind with me and we sorted things out pretty well. I had a new season coming up and with my rib problem still causing me some concern I had to get it checked out. No one at the club gave it too much thought although I kept asking for specialist advice. "Get on with it" was the consensus of opinion, so that's what I did.

# BICKERS

Waqar Younis came back for his second season with the club. With him in the side we felt that we could really win a trophy, preferably the Championship. He was to have a magnificent year, taking 113 Championship wickets at 14 apiece. He took five wickets 13 times in the year, and 10 wickets three times. It was often a privilege to be on the same pitch as him. On his day no one could touch him – a mixture of fast inswinging yorkers and ferocious bouncers causing no end of trouble for the opposition batters. But again, as a team, we came up short. We ended in fifth position as Essex won the title again.

I was still getting too much pain from the rib injury and something clearly wasn't right, so I pulled out of a game against Hampshire. Finally I convinced the club I should have a scan. The scan showed I had actually broken my rib. The muscle had pulled so hard when I tore it that part of my rib had come away with it. An operation was the only answer. Fortunately it wasn't a big job and I only missed a few weeks. The injection I had in Australia clearly hadn't helped. Who was guilty, the medical staff – or me for letting them do it? I would have run through brick walls to play so I went along with anything they suggested.

The problem for the team was that they didn't have enough in reserve when Waqar ran out of gas. After Waqar had finished bowling we lacked penetration in other areas. I struggled with form and fitness again and Keith Medlycott had the onset of the yips, a 'disease' that only seems to affect left-arm spinners. His bowling would never be quite up to the standard that earned him a tour to the West Indies. Batting-wise Darren had another productive year and David Ward carried on from his 1990 form that saw him score over 2,000 runs.

# Martin Bicknell

The Nat West Trophy saw us overcome our jinx of semi-final near misses and get to a final at Lord's. But it nearly didn't get off the ground at all. In the second round we had drawn Oxfordshire, a team of part-timers who 99 times out of 100 we should annihilate. The forecast wasn't looking too good for the two days allocated for the game. We eventually started on day one and were going well before the heavens opened. Coming back to complete the game on the second day we were confronted by incessant rain and puddles everywhere. The dreaded bowl out loomed. Off we trudged into the Indoor School to practice for what now seemed like the inevitable conclusion. We all did OK in practice, apart from Ian Greig who continually fired his deliveries down the leg and into the side netting. He didn't relish the prospect one bit, and made no secret of the fact. All the batsmen fancied their chances of making up the five players selected to do the job. But in more realistic terms the bowlers had to step up.

It was still raining at 5pm and the game was called off. The nightmare scenario was about to take place. Oxfordshire, the equivalent of Accrington Stanley, would go head to head with Surrey of the Premier league. Five bowlers would bowl two balls each at a set of stumps 22 yards away. What struck me at this point was that whoever thought of this solution to a rain-ruined match had no regard for bowlers at all. We have been trained all through our careers to bowl at the 'fourth' stump, down the 'corridor of uncertainty', as Sir Geoffrey likes to call it. And now we had to change what we did naturally and bowl at the bloody stumps.

We selected our five, Bullen, Robinson, Bicknell, Younis and Murphy. Oxfordshire went first and apart from a couple of their guys bowling bouncers they managed to hit twice. We were nervous. Then the twist came. All through practice we had been bowling with old balls, no swing, straight up and down. For the bowl out, just to make it a bit harder for us, we were given brand new balls. For those of you who go to winter nets you will appreciate the fact that new, swinging balls in indoor conditions are a nightmare to control. Well, that's what we found. Chris Bullen, our reliable off spinner, went first and missed twice. Jonny Robinson bowled a bouncer first ball and with his second he almost hit the side net. Over to me; by now I was crapping myself and with quite a few people watching, my hands are getting a little sweaty. I bowl the perfect delivery, to a right hander at the start of a four-day game. Swinging away, just back of a length, unplayable. However the stumps remain intact, unlike my nerves which are now shredded. Second ball I over adjust and the ball doesn't swing and nearly hits the side net. Embarrassed, I sit down and contemplate our early exit from the Nat West Trophy. Up steps Waqar and knocks over the stumps first ball with a ball of extreme pace. He misses with the second and Oxfordshire are rehearsing their winner's song. However, they figured without Tony Murphy. Murph had been great in practice, as had we all, and now it looked as though he was still practising without a care in the world. Up he stepped and hit the stumps first ball. A tie and a potential sudden death. That I didn't need. Second ball and he hits again. Cue Cup final winning celebrations; we scraped through to the next round.

The second round saw us get a home tie against Kent. True to form I dived to my left after three overs to stop a ball from Trevor Ward and my shoulder and I parted company. I knew I was in a bit of trouble but with no real pain I was not sure what was going on. The players all looked a bit concerned and when John Deary, our physio, came on to the field I realised that something must be wrong. As he sat me up I realised my shoulder wasn't where it was supposed to be, but with a quick yank there it was, back in its socket. The pain hit me about two seconds later. Shaking I left the ground to get it sorted out. By the time I got seen at hospital the game was nearly over, not through Surrey's brilliance but because of the endless delay before I saw someone who knew what they were talking about. I got back to the ground all ready to hit the winning runs with one arm. Fortunately I wasn't needed as we cruised home by seven wickets.

The quarter-final gave us Essex at home. It had been three weeks since I dislocated my shoulder and this would be my comeback game. It also saw the opening of the Bedser Stand by the Queen. We met her in between innings. We had posted 253 in our 60 overs but with Gooch in fine form we looked to be out of it until Waqar cleaned him up and I chipped in with a couple of wickets. Under pressure they folded and we had made it into another semi-final. My arm was pretty much hanging off by the end of the game, but it was a gamble that paid off.

So another semi-final, another home tie, this time against Northants. A big crowd came to see us again – more in hope than expectation, so bad was our record in these games. Up until lunch nothing was going to alter their opinion. I walked to the crease about two hours too early at 91-6 and promptly missed my first five deliveries from Paul Taylor, the left-arm seamer. I made an adjustment for the last ball of the over to miss it by a foot, on the outside this time, and the ball hit the middle of my bat. I needed glasses and Surrey needed lunch to regroup. After lunch things got a little easier. The ball was now finding the middle of my bat and we posted a respectable total of 208. Not ground breaking admittedly, but enough to make a game of it. We started poorly with the ball. My heroics with the bat hardly spilled over into my bowling, as Northants reached 68-0. Then Waqar took over. A withering spell of bowling put the game back in the balance as bad light stopped play with Northants requiring 20 to win with just two wickets left. I hardly slept. So near but yet so far. Surely not another near miss on the cards? Waqar tore in for the first ball of the day and dismissed the danger man, Kevin Curran, caught brilliantly by Monte Lynch. A trickle of singles and the occasional two brought the total within range. With eight to win I picked up the ball at mid off and hit the stumps to run the last man out. We had finally done it. This was our final. Just getting to Lord's was enough for us. It didn't matter there was still another game to play; we had broken our nightmare run of semi-final defeats. And boy did we celebrate. Waqar pipped me for the Man of the Match award. I was slightly upset that 66 not out and 2-40 off 12 overs wasn't enough to win the award – plus a run out!

Our season revolved around the Lord's final. It was all we could think about. However, the game before the final would be against Hampshire, our opponents on that day. On a quick wicket Waqar terrorised them, broke Mark Nicholas's hand and made Jon Ayling run away to square leg he was so frightened. We thought we had the measure of them. They feared Waqar and now their captain wouldn't be playing in the final. I managed to pull my groin in the last over of the match and with only four days left to the final it was hardly great timing. Intense physio followed, but in truth I knew I was always going to struggle and it would be touch and go for the big day.

# Martin Bicknell

The morning of the final came around pretty quickly. I headed for the ground early and with all the speculation around my fitness I hardly had time to get nervous. My first fitness test at 8.30am proved I wasn't fit; we had tried everything. As a last resort we tried acupuncture, hardly my favourite form of treatment but I was prepared to give it a go. Well – work it did, the muscles around my groin relaxed and I declared myself fit. Hampshire won the toss and a big roar went around the ground. It was almost traditional that if you won the toss you bowled first, and such was the success ratio between teams winning the toss and winning the game that we were apprehensive to say the least. In a way, that probably epitomised our approach. In the first half of our innings, we crawled along before a mixture of Thorpe, Ward and Stewart rallied us to 240-5. In reply Hampshire got off to a great start before we inched our way back into the game. With three overs to go they needed 22 to win. Tony Murphy was entrusted with the third to last over, Waqar would bowl the next and then I would bowl the last. It couldn't be any tighter. Jon Ayling was batting. Bearing in mind he had been so scared of Waqar the week before, Murph thought he was quick enough to bounce him. Mistake number one. Short and wide, and Ayling despatched it into the stand for six. If that wasn't bad enough, the next ball he pitched up and Ayling hit it straight at Ian Greig at mid on. Mistake number two. With almost comic timing Ian let it through his legs for four. Effectively game over in two balls. It went to the final over, but off the second last ball Hampshire were crowned Nat West Champions. We took second spot.

It was a complete let down. People talk about the final being a great day out. It is if you win. We were gutted. The after-match meal we planned as a celebration was a waste of time. We drowned our sorrows all the same and talked about what might have been.

Off the pitch my life was like a soap opera. Rebecca had come over but not settled at all. I guess it was a bit much to ask her to leave her country of birth and move to a place where she knew only me. She was totally dependent on me and I couldn't handle it. After a couple of months we split and she went back to Perth. Shortly afterwards I found myself back with Emma. Don't really know how that happened but it only lasted a couple of weeks before we both realised it wasn't going to work. Shortly after that I found myself back on the phone to Rebecca in Perth. I really have no idea what I was doing, apart from messing with people's lives. It was embarrassing. A team-mate at the time, Rehan Alikhan, was getting married in Perth of all places and I was invited. I spoke to Rebecca about it and she said I could stay with her. I had made my mind up now and I wanted Rebecca back in my life. I travelled to Perth for the December wedding and we got back together. You couldn't make up a story like that.

I had been selected for the winter tour to the West Indies with the England A team. I came back from Australia on my own; Rebecca would come over in the summer. I moved into a three-bedroomed house in Sutton and life was good for a while. In the first practice session for the tour I ran up to bowl and in my delivery stride my shoulder popped out again. It didn't feel that serious though, there was no real pain and it popped back in easily. I bowled two days later, without any concern. However, the England Cricket Board said they weren't prepared to take a chance with me and I was to have an operation to fix the problem. No tour, only months of rehab to follow. The operation was long and the recovery painful. I watched the World Cup from the comfort of my new sofa; I walked around the house unable to use my left arm at all. Living on your own can be a nightmare at the best of times. Try doing it with one arm. The winter dragged on and on. Slowly I got the use of my arm back but it wasn't until mid-April before I could bowl again.

Surrey had made a couple of new signings for the 1992 season. Joey Benjamin came from Warwickshire and Rudi Bryson was our overseas player. Rudi was from South Africa and not the sharpest tool in the box. We all lived together for a while. Joey rented my spare room and Rudi lived with us for a month. Rudi just wanted to party hard. He drank more beers than he bowled overs throughout the season. It wasn't the greatest of signings, especially after Waqar. Bryson took just 17 wickets in the Championship, at an average of 68. Waqar had gone back to terrorise the English batsmen on the Pakistani tour to England. Both he and Wasim Akram destroyed England that year. Ball tampering was the only topic of conversation. Balls were roughed up much in the same way as they had been at Surrey, but this time, more in the public eye. It was an unpleasant tour.

With a poor overseas signing our season never got going. Personally I had a great year and ended with 67 wickets and over 400 runs in the Championship. I was now on the brink of becoming an all rounder. After the initial nightmare start to my career with the bat, I had worked out which end of the bat to hold. I think what had helped was the move away from the fast overseas West Indian bowlers to all rounders and spinners. I was terrorised as soon as I turned professional, barraged with short balls that I had never faced before. I couldn't cope and my confidence drained. In one match against Hampshire Malcolm Marshall illustrated the point perfectly. First ball was a bouncer that flew just past my nose. Second up was an outswinger. With my feet rooted to the spot I missed it by miles. Then the killer ball, the fast inswinger, stumps everywhere, job done. It was basic cricket, executed perfectly by one of the greatest of all time. Scare the life out of someone first; then get him out.

I really wasn't that into my batting. I adopted the 'best when fresh' mentality, rarely venturing into the nets. I guess I just had the fear of being hit all the time. I didn't play bouncers overly well, although I did get better and improved over time. But the really quick guys were always going to be an issue. Many times I walked to the middle thinking I was about to be cleaned up. Some bowlers gave me sleepless nights. Courtney Walsh on a bouncy wicket at Cheltenham was just a nightmare, as was Mohammed Sami. Dave Fulton, the Kent captain had great pleasure in adapting the bodyline theory for my benefit in a game at The Oval. I had scored my first hundred against them a year before. I wasn't about to be gifted any more cover drives.

I always found batsmen fascinating, especially what they did with their bats. For most of us, we got sent our bats at the start of the season and generally if they looked alright and picked up well that would be it – use it. Not Ramprakash or Thorpe. So obsessed were they with finding the right handle, thickness, and feel, that they would spend hours taking the string off the handle, applying little bits of tape, and restringing the bat. A grip would then go on and the work would be inspected. If it still didn't feel right the whole process would start again. It had to be perfect. They had different bats for one-day games, one for white balls, one for red balls, one for the end of an innings, for low wickets and for fast, bouncy ones.

# Martin Bicknell

It was all so confusing. I generally had one good one. It was the bat for all occasions. I didn't have a choice.

The antics of a batter always intrigued me too. Over the course of a season you get your fair share of good and bad decisions. Plenty of times a batsmen will 'get away with it', nick one or be stone dead on an LBW decision. Nothing is generally said about that. When a batsman gets a poor decision though, all hell breaks loose, bats are thrown, kit goes flying and the umpire is called all the names under the sun. Ramprakash regularly thought certain umpires had a vendetta against him, but in recent years he hasn't got out enough to sustain that opinion anymore.

Things were looking up off the field. I got engaged to Rebecca and life was good. She had brought a friend with her this time to help her settle and we got on much better. It wasn't a relationship built on the firmest of foundations though and we regularly argued over the smallest things. We agreed to get married the following November which gave us a good year to see if things could go wrong, again!

I spent the winter of 1992 back in Perth, this time playing some cricket and working on my fitness. I picked out a club; they paid my air fare and a little spending money. The club was right next to Swanbourne beach, famous for nude sun bathers, so we had a good eyeful for most of the season. The cricket was played hard, as you would expect, and I copped the usual shed load of abuse every time I walked to the crease. It was your normal anti-English banter apart from one day when this guy started insulting the Queen. I'm not sure he was bright enough to realise she was in fact their Queen too. Most of it was good natured and I ended up giving quite a bit back. I managed my first hundred and took a few wickets. It was a good winter.

# BICKERS

I couldn't get through an entire season without some form of injury though. We had a lad called Ian Houseman who had played for Yorkshire. He could bowl fast but with a tendency to spray it round a bit. I was batting against him in the nets and for some reason wasn't wearing a helmet. He bowled a ball slightly back of a length. I moved back and across and got myself into line. The nets had a slight ridge in them and every now and again the ball would rear up at you. Well, this ball did exactly that. As I raised my gloves in front of my face I could see this red kookaburra ball appearing in front of my eyes. The next thing I know I am in the corner of the net with blood all over the place. The ball crashed straight into my nose, splitting it down the middle. In situations like that you know that, well-meaning as people are, they haven't got a clue about first aid. They applied an ice pack to my head and took me to casualty. I was in all sorts of pain and with blood streaming from my nose. All that was happening was that the ice pack had now stuck to my face. Taking it off only made the cut worse. The nurse stitched me back up and I left the hospital with a head the size of a football. All the colours of the rainbow were nicely represented on my face. It wasn't a pretty sight. I missed a game, which in Australia meant two weeks, and I didn't bat without a helmet again.

I left Perth, nicely tanned and with a positive mind. Training had gone really well, and my cricket was good. I had managed to do some work with Dennis Lillee too. He was a bundle of energy and you could only be impressed by his approach to the game. He still played, trained hard and helped people out. His affection for the game was contagious. The couple of sessions I did with him were priceless. Little did we both know I would be playing against his countrymen later in the year.

# Test Call-Up At Last

I had a couple of good years after the tour to Australia in 1990-91. However I still had some injuries which set me back a little. But when I did play I felt I was getting better and better, more confident and maturing as a cricketer. It was almost as if I had to go back to county cricket and really learn my trade before I earned my way back into the reckoning for England.

Despite getting to 50 championship wickets faster than anyone else, I still felt the selectors weren't convinced about me. This seemed to be confirmed by the fact that even though England kept being hammered out of sight by Australia and using a record number of players, I still hadn't had the call. Lack of pace had been held against me throughout my career and this infuriated me whenever I heard it mentioned. I was getting good players out – top order players, Test players. If I could do it at county level then why couldn't I do it on the biggest stage? It frustrates me to think that I missed so much Test cricket while our selectors kept on searching for 90mph bowlers. Surely it doesn't matter what speed you bowl if you get the best players out, does it?

Finally the call came. The Trent Bridge squad was announced and my name was in it. I found out that I was in the squad by the traditional method of looking at Ceefax on the TV at around 11am on Sunday morning. It had finally happened, a Test call-up. The sense of relief after waiting so long was overwhelming and I was on my way to Nottingham. I didn't really believe I was going to play, but to be in the squad was good enough for me at this stage. Being in the England side is so different from turning out for your county. The endless freebies, someone carrying your bag, nice expenses; I could get used to this, I thought! What I wasn't really expecting though was the press attention and the countless interviews.

The press attention and the glare of the spotlight can do funny things to players. That is why you sometimes never see the best of players who should be world beaters. Some people just cannot handle the pressure that goes with playing for England and being in the public eye. I guess Graeme Hick is the most spectacular example of what expectations can do to a player. When Hick first came into county cricket he dominated to such an extent that everyone thought that once he had served his qualification period he would be a massive star on the world stage. However his introduction to Test cricket was against the West Indies and he didn't get off to the greatest start. Hick would probably admit that he never really did himself justice in an England shirt.

The team was finally announced on the morning of the game and I found myself on the way back down the M1, surplus to requirements. It was disappointing, but I knew I was next cab off the rank. I went back to Surrey and took another eight wickets in the demolition of Durham. I was in the form of my life. I was ready.

The fourth Test at Headingley was on the horizon. England had just drawn the last one at Trent Bridge and traditionally the Yorkshire venue would favour the English type of bowler. The question was, would England play four seam bowlers and leave out the spinner? There were injuries around too. I was pretty sure I was going to get a game this time. It felt real.

Now the nerves really start to kick in. I don't know whether I am going to play but I make my way up north with a sense of excitement and fear. I am desperate to play, but am I good enough? Am I good enough to bowl at Steve Waugh, Allan Border and Mark Taylor? What will it be like facing Shane Warne? It is a fear that I have faced my entire career. I don't think I am the most confident of people. Despite a great record in the game, I still have this underlying fear that I could mess up at any stage. All I can think about is bowling the first ball of my Test career and not making a fool of myself. I don't want to let people down and get smashed all over Headingley, do I?

The build up to the game continues over the Tuesday and Wednesday. Keith Fletcher is manager and Graham Gooch, a man under real pressure, is captain. After going to Australia with Graham as captain I know to expect a dour character who doesn't say much. But now I am pleasantly surprised. He has changed. A recent divorce and a new partner seem to have given him a sunnier outlook and we get on quite well. There is not much belief in the camp though. A frequently changing side – senior players who have been losing to Australia for a while on the one hand and young nervous players on the other, don't add up to a team expecting to win. English cricket is in transition and I would like to be part of the new crop of players to take England forward. Just wish it wasn't against Australia!

I am fortunate to know quite a few of the other players in the squad. Mark Illott and Martin McCague, two of the other seam bowlers, I know quite well. Two others I am not too sure about. Andrew Caddick, potentially at this stage a fine bowler in the making, is in the team but has yet to make his mark at this level. There are real question marks about him as a person – something he would have to contend with for his whole career. Personally I always rated him very highly but found him a bit of an oddball. He seemed to have this insecurity about fitting in. Maybe it was his New Zealand background that gave him a sense of not belonging to the team and he felt he had to try extra hard to be 'one of the lads'. I know this wound a lot of people up and he wasn't the most popular player on the circuit. Darren Gough had real issues with him. Maybe that spurred them both on when they played together for England. It would be fair to say they shared a mutual dislike!

The other player I didn't really know that well was Mark Lathwell, a very talented opening batsman from Somerset who looked like a fish out of water away from his beloved cider county. The entire time we were together I honestly didn't hear him speak once. I think he found the whole event just too overwhelming, with the result that England never had a chance to see the best of this really talented player. Early the next year he and I went on the ill-fated South African tour together with the England A team. I roomed with him early on that trip and although I did get to hear him speak it was clear that he hated every minute away from the West Country. It was no real surprise that his career faded quickly and he retired at a very early age. Can you imagine an Australian being like that? We don't breed them tough in this country.

Thursday morning and it's the first day of the Test. There is a full house – more in hope than expectation of an England win. I get the nod to play as Peter Such, our spinner, is left out to accommodate four seamers. It's always a risky move to leave out your spinner in a Test match, but do I care? No, I am playing Test cricket for England and amid my excitement I am crapping myself. We lose the toss and on a good-looking Headingley wicket, and Australia choose to bat. Bloody hell, I have to bowl soon! We open the bowling with McCague and Illott and Australia are off to a flyer. Martin McCague didn't have that great an England career. For a guy with an Australian upbringing he opted out too often for people's liking when the going got tough. This game was no different and after a while he limped off with a back injury. It is always hard to assess a player's injury. Some players have higher pain thresholds than others and go through the pain for the team. Others take the easy option and walk away. I guess you never really know how much another player can deal with, injury wise. Some injuries just get worse the more you play, others take a little bit of courage to play on. But after a few years you can spot the guys with big hearts.

My chance came soon enough. Gooch told me to get loose and replace the ineffective McCague from the Kirkstall End. Talk about nervous now.

My first ball and first over passed in a blur. I felt good though and the ball was coming out nicely with a bit of swing. In my third over my dream came true. Mark Taylor, the prolific Aussie opener, became my first Test wicket. A nice bit of late swing back into the pads of the left-hander and umpire Nigel Plews had no doubt that it was going to hit the stumps. That was it, a Test wicket, and a pretty good one at that. Surely this was the start of something great? I would carry on, take five wickets and inspire England to a great victory over the old enemy.

# BICKERS

Alas, no; fairy tales don't happen that often in sport do they? If someone had told me I would have to wait another 65 overs for my next Test wicket I would have told them they were having a laugh. But it was true. Australia batted well into the third day and totalled 650-4. Allan Border scored 200 and Steve Waugh 150. They never looked like getting out but I did manage to get consecutive balls past Border's bat, a real success. Actually I bowled very well during my 50 overs. True, I only took one wicket for 155 runs, but it was widely accepted that I was the pick of the English bowlers and word was that I was going to stay in the side for the next Test at Edgbaston. However, we still had work to do chasing Australia's score. But this was not a good England side. The innings defeat came as no real surprise to anyone, nor did the resignation of Graham Gooch as another Ashes series was lost to the rampant Aussies.

Perhaps Keith Fletcher should have gone too? What he brought to the England side really wasn't that clear to me. My experience in Kenya and Zimbabwe hadn't left me with a positive feeling towards him. Here at Headingley I got a similar impression. For a man with such a great reputation at Essex he really didn't pull up too many trees at this level. Mike Atherton was named as the new captain and we moved on to Edgbaston. More changes to the England side followed. Out went Caddick, McCague and Lathwell and in came Matt Maynard, Peter Such and an ageing John Emburey. The reason John came back was that when we got to Birmingham to see the pitch it looked like a spinner's dream. Right up Shane Warne's street in fact. Only in England can we be so helpful to touring sides.

We won what we thought was a good toss and made a bit of a hash of

# Martin Bicknell

it. Paul Reiffel, a bowler similar to me, took five wickets for the Aussies and we were bowled out on day one for a below par score. When it came to our turn to bowl I felt much more confident than I had in the first Test and a real sense that I belonged at this level. My 3-99 off over 35 overs represented a really good effort, the wickets of Steve Waugh, Ian Healy and Merv Hughes capping a good display. During the innings I had a great run in with Steve Waugh. Steve had a reputation as a real fighter but not as a great player of the short ball, so I gave it everything. The crowd sensed a real battle was going on and got behind me. I loved it, being the centre of attention, getting stuck into an Aussie. This is what I was playing Test cricket for. Come the end of the day though, I felt mentally drained. The words I had with the still not out Waugh meant that tomorrow would have plenty riding on it.

That evening I went out with a friend for a meal into the centre of Birmingham. You can imagine my surprise when, as I walked in, who should be in the restaurant and, as it turned out, sitting on an adjoining table? Yep, Steve Waugh and his wife! We exchanged glances, had a little smile and carried on with our food. Life can be pretty strange. The next morning I was thrown the ball at the start of the day and soon found the edge of Waugh's bat. I had my man and I let him know it too. Bloody hell, this felt good. I felt like the main man. Even though we performed much better than at Headingley we lost again. Shane Warne and Tim May found the turning surface to their liking and another defeat to Australia followed.

On the positive side I was a certainty for the last Test of the summer on my home ground at The Oval. I felt really comfortable in the side now and was even looking forward to the winter tour to the West Indies. One more good performance should seal my tour place. Well that was the idea.

In between the Test matches I had a Surrey match at Worcester. Nowadays, in the era of central contracts, I would not have played. I would have rested up for the last Test to avoid any sort of injury or tiredness. As it was I played at Worcester and carried on my great run in county cricket that season, taking another 11 wickets. Unfortunately I bowled 65 overs in the process and by the end of the game I was hobbling in with a knee problem that had been getting gradually worse. I was knackered too and I knew that my chances of playing at The Oval were fading fast.

Looking back, if I had been a bit more selfish I wouldn't have put myself in a position to bowl so many overs. The game was very important to Surrey though and a possible Championship title was on the line, so I did everything in my power to win. As it was we lost the game and I bowled myself into hospital and a rendez-vous with the surgeon's knife. Perhaps it wouldn't have happened if I had only bowled half the overs I did, but that wasn't how I played for Surrey. I was desperate for the team to win something. But again the season ended with nothing to show for our efforts.

I reported to The Oval and went straight to the physio. The diagnosis wasn't great and an operation to repair my damaged patella tendon was almost a certainty. Nevertheless I thought I had done more than enough to make the tour party in January. But during that Test, Angus Fraser returned after a long absence through injury. Steve Watkin, the Glamorgan seamer, took a few wickets and England won the match. I knew now my tour place would not be a certainty and when it was announced that I would not be going on the main tour, but instead to South Africa with the A team, I lost it.

It's really difficult to describe the feeling of rejection I experienced, but needless to say I didn't handle it very well. I was out for the season so I might as well go off the rails for a while. Putting it into context, I played 10 first-class games that season for Surrey and took 63 wickets at 17 runs apiece. I played two Tests, and by the end of those two Tests I was the leading seam bowler in the side, going into the last game at The Oval. You can see why I was a little disappointed!

I remember the day the squad was announced only too clearly. There were no phone calls back then and no communication from the selectors, so you found out at the same time as the general public. The Surrey boys were at a benefit function for Alec Stewart at Sandown Racecourse, having a couple of beers and enjoying the racing. For some reason the England squad was announced on the PA system and thinking I would be going, I got a massive shock when I didn't hear my name. It wouldn't be the last time I didn't hear my name on a team sheet in my career, so there was only one thing for it I thought. Get hammered. It wasn't just for the one day either. Being a single man back then with no one to rein me in and time to kill, I carried on for a few weeks before I got it partially out of my system. It was unprofessional – I knew that. But I was gutted. I knew I was good enough to play for England and the selectors were robbing me of my opportunity. Little was I to know it would be another 10 years before I got another chance.

My relationship issues were still a nightmare. Rebecca had come over to England and once again we weren't getting on. For the three months she

# BICKERS

was over we just argued. I looked forward to her going home to be honest. We were still getting married though. Plans were in full swing for a November wedding in Perth. The church was booked, as was the reception. When Rebecca left I breathed a huge sigh of relief. I started to enjoy myself again, unburdened by the pressure of an intense relationship. We still argued of course, but now it was over the phone. It dawned on me that I was not happy in this relationship and I had to do something about it. There weren't too many options. The wedding planning had to stop; I was not going to marry someone I couldn't get on with. It led to me calling her and telling her it was all over. Not the best way of dealing with things I know but it's what I had to do. It wasn't possible for me to go over and tell her mid season so the phone was the only option. It was weak but I didn't know what else to do. She called me nonstop after that, in the middle of the night, during Test matches and her Mother even called me. I really felt for her. I sure as hell wouldn't have appreciated someone doing that to me. In hindsight I should have told her before she left but it didn't feel the right thing to do. I needed some time on my own to get my head around things, to understand my true feelings towards her. I handled it poorly.

The knee operation came and went, rehab followed and the tour to South Africa wasn't until December so I had a 'good time' for a while. At the end of that summer, just before I went to South Africa, I met Loraine at a Surrey function. We would eventually get married in September 1995. However, at the time it didn't really change my outlook on life too much and I headed to South Africa with a sore knee and determined to enjoy myself. I still thought if I went to South Africa and did well I might get a chance in the West Indies if someone got injured. Things didn't quite turn out the way I planned it however. I did manage to damage my reputation though.

I was still smarting from the non-selection for the main tour when we left for South Africa. I still had knee problems as well, though I thought these would get better in time and I would be able to bowl full on towards the end of the tour. I should never have gone. Early net sessions proved I was nowhere near fit and I missed the early games. Missing games for me meant going out and having a few beers. I latched on to Dominic Cork and we were out most nights, not doing enough rehab and letting myself go. I don't really know what got into me but I was out of control. The management knew it too. They could see I was not looking after myself properly. Phil Neale, now part of the England setup and a lovely guy, subtly tried to rein me in, to get me training properly and look after myself a bit better. I was more interested in having a good time and the next round of golf.

Eventually I got fit enough to play. The Boxing Day match at Cape Town would be a huge occasion and I felt I was ready. Training had gone well and for some strange reason I thought I was a racing certainty to stroll back into the side at the expense of others who had performed really well on the tour so far. Well, they left me out. Again I wasn't happy but I should have seen it coming. Eventually I did get my chance – in the next game.

We moved on up to Durban for New Year. South Africa was coming out of apartheid and was still quite a sensitive place to be. We were the first touring side back in the country and while we were led to believe that touring South Africa would be similar to touring Australia that claim was way off the mark. When we arrived in Johannesburg at the start of the tour we were told we were entering the second highest murder capital in the world and if possible we should try and avoid going out at night. It wasn't what I was expecting, and it wasn't Australia! I felt uncomfortable throughout the whole tour; although apartheid had been lifted there were still far too many reminders of how life used to be. It was clear that the white South Africans were still coming to terms with sharing a restaurant with people who used to clean their shoes on the pavements. Durban on New Year's Day saw 100,000 black Africans on the beach. It was an intimidating atmosphere, and I wanted to get out as soon as I could.

The game in Durban signalled the end of my tour. We lost the toss and bowled first. I took the new ball and after three overs I pulled my side muscle so badly I could hardly walk, let alone bowl. I walked off the pitch and out of the tour. The whole trip had been a disaster. I had let myself down; the injury was probably caused by my body trying to compensate for my knee injury. Later I would hear that my tour report wasn't crash hot either. I would have to wait nearly 10 years to get back into England colours.

# Barren Times

Coming off the back of the 1994 tour to South Africa my head wasn't in the right place. I was still smarting from the England snub, and now I had this nasty side injury to contend with as well. An injury that happened on 1st January was still giving me cause for concern three months later.

It was all change at the club too. Geoff Arnold, the man responsible for looking after my bowling action was sacked. It was a hammer blow to me and many of the players he had nurtured in their formative years. Arnold had paid the price for the club's years of underachieving. Not really his fault – more that of the players at his disposal. He was never really a Committee man either, his abrasive style not suited to the men in suits.

In his place came Graham Clinton and Mike Edwards, along with Graham Dilley as second-team coach. If the club was looking for the dream team for success I am not sure it was these guys. Clinton I knew very well from my early playing days at the club. Clint could be an odd character but I found him hilarious at times. He had visited just about every A&E hospital in England. Being an opening batsman in the 1980s was a fairly hazardous occupation. It was still the era of the West Indian quick bowler and taking blows on the body was part of the job. Clint took more than his fair share. If he had been a boxer he would have spent most days taking the compulsory eight count. As a player he was very limited, but made the most of his ability. He served Surrey well. He had been second-team coach and had done well in that environment. However, the step up to first-team coach caused him problems. He was good in the young players' environment in the second team, but his style of coaching just wasn't suited to senior players.

Mike Edwards ran youth cricket at Surrey for as long as anyone could remember. He had been in charge of the Surrey Young Cricketers when I played and that was really his scene. I don't think he ever wanted the job as cricket manager but the club talked him into it. Mike had been out of the game for too long and didn't know anything about the current crop of players. At least when he stepped down after a couple of years the club had the decency to give him his old job back. As for Graham Dilley, I didn't really know him at all. An outstanding fast bowler in his time, I was really looking forward to working with him. I still wanted to improve as a bowler; I wanted that extra yard of pace everyone kept talking about. I hoped he might be able to add that to my game – whereas he was of the opinion that 'if it ain't broke, don't try and fix it'. I was gradually coming round to the view that I was never going to find that extra yard. Fast bowlers are born not made. I was going to have to settle for skill rather than brute force.

As I was now a senior player at the club I was appointed vice-captain to Alec. I was looking forward to the challenge, and I knew with Alec's commitments with England I would have the opportunity to captain the side. My captaincy experience was virtually zero though but it couldn't be that hard, could it?

We got off to an absolute flyer in all competitions. We won the first three matches in the Championship and progressed well in the Benson and Hedges. There was a real feeling that this could be our year. We had new players really making their mark. Adam Hollioake, Mark Butcher, Joey Benjamin and Cameron Cuffy were the up and coming stars of the team. The more established players like me and Darren, Graham Thorpe, Ali Brown and David Ward marked us out as a new force in the game. The area we were short in was spin. Neil Kendrick, Andy Smith and James Boiling shared that responsibility, but they weren't going to win you that many games. We still thought we had enough fire power though. All we had to do was convert our performances into results and trophies.

An early test of my captaincy came at home to Northants. After winning the first three games I wanted the run to continue. I gambled a bit on our declaration and set them just over 300 in nearly 90 overs. We lost by three wickets. Zero from one on my CV.

I was having my usual struggle on the injury front though. My knee operation from the previous winter hadn't gone as well as expected and it was still sore. Whether it contributed to my next problem I'm not sure. In the quarter-final of the Benson and Hedges in Nottingham I felt a really sharp pain in my right foot. It came as I bowled my final ball so I just walked off the ground to the usual cry of "go and put your feet up now you have finished your bowling". I knew I was in a bit of bother though. The physio sent me straight to the local sports clinic and the x-ray revealed a stress fracture. No cricket for six weeks, no walking for at least two.

Bored senseless after a couple of weeks, all I could do was watch as we crashed out of another semi-final, this time to Warwickshire. We batted first and got to a decent score, and in reply Warwickshire struggled for a while to chase it down. Then came Brian Lara at number six, fresh from making 401 not out the previous day against Durham; he was tired so he dropped down the order, but that didn't stop him flaying the Surrey bowling all over Kennington. Lara showed all his class with a brilliant 70. It was a game we probably should have won, and if it hadn't been for Lara we would have, but it was another defeat in a semi. It was getting a bit depressing. I amused myself during my time off by eating and drinking too much, not doing enough training and watching television in the dressing room. I was on a bit of a downward spiral.

I made my comeback on 3rd July in a Sunday League game at Durham. I had trained for a couple of days before the match to test the foot and it felt OK. In the game I felt rusty, unfit and off the pace. It was my first win as captain though, albeit in a one-day game. During my time away from the game I had slid down the pecking order. Cameron Cuffy and Joey Benjamin had performed excellently and with Tony Piggott also bowling well there was an established look to our team. In Hollioake and Butcher we had two good all rounders. Our next Championship game was at Guildford. I hadn't played for a few weeks but I thought it was still a formality I would be selected. After all I had played for England only last year. I got onto the field and joined Clinton and Alec Stewart to discuss the team line-up. As vice-captain I thought my input was always necessary! When it came to the bowlers Alec said it was two from three to fill the last two spots. It was between me, Piggott and Benjamin. He then asked me how I was bowling. It all clicked in my head at this point. He wanted me to say things hadn't been going that well and in all probability I shouldn't play. That was never going to happen. After a heated discussion I was told. I left the ground in a massive strop. I wasn't going to hang around and be twelfth man. That was beneath me. I was fuming as I drove out of the ground, seething at the injustice of it all.

I had gone from England's opening bowler to 2nd XI in the space of just under a year. This wasn't supposed to happen. I was vice-captain and one of the senior players at the club. How could they treat me like this? In truth I was behaving like a spoilt brat. Another injury soon followed. I wasn't looking after myself very well. I had put on weight and rehab was a nasty word. No one was going to tell me what to do. I knew it all.

Another incident at The Oval really summed up the person I had become. I had two lockers at the time, not sure why, but I managed to spread all my belongings over the two. Adam Hollioake had just been capped, an honour that meant he would be able to come into our changing room. As all the lockers were allocated my second one would be his. All this happened when I wasn't at the ground. The day I came in and saw my stuff had been moved out I once again behaved like a spoilt child. I created so much fuss Adam just picked up his things and went straight back to where he had come from. I am embarrassed when I look back at it now. I was selfish, arrogant and an idiot.

Yet another comeback followed, this time in the Sunday League game against Sussex at The Oval. I bowled OK, and with the Nat West semi-final a couple of days away I had to get a game in if I wanted to play. In the quarter-final of the Nat West against Glamorgan, Tony Murphy, now a fringe player, had taken 6-26 in 12 overs, won Man of the Match and established his place in the team for the semi. Or so he thought. With me coming back from injury the selection team had an issue. It was down to me or Murph. I got the nod, much to my delight, but not his. He quite rightly lost it, smashed his locker door in and stormed out of the ground. He only came back to the ground to collect his belongings. He had played his last game for the club. Murph had done so much for Surrey that it was a real shame it had to end that way.

In truth he probably did well to miss the match. After Joey Benjamin had taken a couple of early wickets we chased the ball all over Kennington. Tim Curtis, who would normally make Chris Tavaré look exciting, smashed 136, and Tom Moody hit an unbeaten 180. Standing down at long on felt like being at the end of a golf driving range. A total of 357-2 in 60 overs was way out of our reach, so we thought. We started well, and the rate didn't really climb significantly. We lost wickets at regular intervals though and despite great innings from Hollioake and Brown we looked out of it. However, there was still plenty of fight in James Boiling and Joey Benjamin. With 19 needed off the last four balls Benjamin deposited the first two, way back for six. Seven off two balls was still possible and Benjamin once again wound up like Babe Ruth. The ball looked certain to clear the ropes again until the 9' 10" figure of Tom Moody took it high above his head at long off. It was all over, another semi-final, another defeat.

The Championship wheels were falling off too with our lack of quality spin causing us no end of problems. I was back in the side, and as captain for the trip to Southampton. The team had been playing poorly for a while now and this game would be no exception. I won the toss on a flat, dry looking pitch. After an hour we were 48-6 against some really innocuous bowling. It was pitiful. 150 all out was a fair indictment of where we were at. It got much worse. Cameron Cuffy took a wicket in the first over of our reply and then walked off the ground complaining of a sore shoulder. It left me and the spinners to bowl. Neil Kendrick toiled manfully for 40 overs. He did however have a habit of spitting at opposition batsmen, a habit that didn't endear him to the opposition fast bowlers. He knew how to wind people up. We played in a game against Lancashire at The Oval and when Kendrick had bowled to Wasim Akram there was a bit of an altercation. Akram was not amused. I batted ahead of Kendrick when we batted, and with Akram going through the motions all seemed well. We lost a wicket and in came Kendrick. Akram slipped a couple of gears and broke Kendrick's toe, scaring the life out of me by trying to kill me in the process as well. And none of it was my fault!

Back at Southampton things weren't going well. I used nine bowlers including five spinners, the best of whom being Darren, who came on for one over before the declaration. That said it all. Hampshire scored 603-7 and we lost by an innings and 68. Mark Butcher did score his maiden first-class hundred in a losing cause. Zero from two on my CV. It soon became zero from three as we played Middlesex. Conscious of my earlier error in setting a low total to chase against Northants, I erred on the side of caution. I set Middlesex 390 to win in 84 overs. Gatting and Ramprakash hit us all over the shop. We had given up playing spinners at this stage of the season, so our all seam attack was a bit one-paced – and average to say the least.

One bright spot for me came at Scarborough as I finally produced something to take five wickets in the second innings against Yorkshire. It proved to me I could still bowl, when fit. It was a good performance considering I had only had two hours sleep as well. The Surrey card school was still going strong – Brown , Bicknell, Ward and Piggott regularly playing during away trips into the early hours. I guess it stopped us going out drinking and partying. This particular night we didn't have a great sense of time keeping and before we knew it, it was 4am. A couple more, 'last hands' and it was 5am. By the time we got to bed it was nearly time to get up. Next morning came too early, but feeling strongly that I didn't want to let my team-mates down I reeled off 21 overs to demonstrate that maybe after all I didn't need any sleep to play cricket. I did put that theory to the test once, in a game at Durham in 1992. We played all night. It got to 6am and we had a choice – get a solid one hour's sleep or try and recoup some of your lost money? It was a bit of a no brainer to be honest. Breakfast with dark glasses on once again was a bit of a giveaway so we avoided it. And with that sense of 'maybe my preparation wasn't quite right' I took five wickets again giving it all I'd got. I slept well the next night though.

The gambling drug can be too much sometimes, especially for sportsmen with more time and money than they know what to do with. I have been close to 'not knowing when to stop' and it remains a weakness for me. I tend to go through periods where I gamble and it can get a bit heavy at times. But I can also stop myself. I'm a little bit all or nothing. I can get consumed by things, and then walk away. My personality is like that. I can play chess for example, for a month on end, every day and it becomes a real drug. Then I will get bored and stop, and move onto something else. Life can be a bit tedious sometimes and these little addictions give me something to focus on.

The 1994 season had died a death. Another year of 'so near and yet so far' for the Surrey faithful. I had managed the grand total of eight games in the Championship. It was a season wrecked by injury and poor attitude. I had discovered I could put on weight, that I was being a bit of an arsehole and that I wasn't the greatest captain in the world. I was further away from the England setup than ever and wasn't even the best bowler at the club. Joey Benjamin by taking 76 wickets had played against South Africa in the last Test of the summer and got himself on the tour to Australia. I was glad the season was over.

The off season gave me the chance to get myself really fit again. Seeing myself on TV with an arse the size of Guildford gave me the perfect incentive to work hard and get myself back into shape. I lost a shed load of weight, trained hard and approached 1995 with a fresh attitude. We left for Perth on 1st April for pre-season. With perfect timing Loraine gave birth to Ellie on 31st March so I could catch the flight. Perth wouldn't have been my ideal location for pre-season. Since I had told Rebecca on the phone we weren't going to get married, my name was mud all over Perth. I was expecting the worst – for someone to come out from a dark corner and hit me. I was at least expecting to see her, but it didn't happen.

The cricket in Perth went brilliantly; I was fit, strong and thinner. For the first time in a couple of years I had no injury concerns and the season couldn't come round quick enough. Cuffy had left and in would come Carl Rackemann, an enormous hulk of a man with an appetite for alcohol that knew no bounds. Nadeem Shahid came from Essex and Jason Ratcliffe from Warwickshire and the squad was assembled. Spin was once again a massive concern. Richard Nowell, a left-arm spinner, joined from the young cricketers but he wasn't going to win you a Championship.

Pre-season couldn't have gone any better, but right on cue I got injured on day one of the season. I pulled up with a calf injury in mid-run as if someone had shot me from the nearby flats. We won the game however and were on our way. I reappeared a couple of weeks later in the win against Durham at The Oval. My form was good; I just couldn't stay on the pitch. First it was a calf injury and then it was my hamstring. The hamstring injury was bizarre to say the least. I would injure it in a game, go through the rehab and treatment, get it right again, and then it would go again. This happened three times. As frustrated as I was about missing games of cricket, the management took on a different view. Surrey were playing at Horsham against Sussex. I wasn't playing as usual, but a phone call from Graham Clinton summoned me down to the ground. Clearly I had been the topic of much debate amongst Alec Stewart and Clinton. This meeting broke new ground for me when Alec asked me if I was imagining I was injured. He thought I might have become the next Paul Jarvis – apparently he always thought he was injured when he wasn't. My jaw dropped a little lower. This coming from someone I really respected as well. Did they really think I was feigning injury? Did they think I was enjoying not playing? Fuming, I left the ground. I spoke to the physio, who at this stage wasn't speaking to Clinton because of an earlier argument. He sent me off for a scan at my request. The scan showed I had a cyst in my hamstring that was causing me to pull the muscle every time I put it under stress. An operation was the only option, to remove the cyst and let the muscle work properly. More time off followed. No apology from the management for accusing me of faking injury though.

I think the pressure of the job had really got to Clinton. He didn't get on that well with Mike Edwards, had no contact with the physio, and alienated some of the senior players by his treatment of them. One of the only sensible things he did was to appoint Adam Hollioake as captain in my and Alec's absence. Adam was turning into a top performer and although he didn't immediately strike you as captaincy material he sure as hell turned into a fine one. An early sign of it came in the match against Yorkshire at The Oval. The game had been going Yorkshire's way for a while and with 218 to win in the second innings it looked a formality. It looked even more of a formality when Yorkshire were 185-3 and cruising. Only one man thought the impossible was possible. Bringing himself on to bowl he took 4-22 in 10 overs. Clever field placements, inspired bowling changes and an incredible desire to chase lost causes won Surrey the match by one run. Hollioake had arrived as a captain.

The 1995 season saw the beginning of Alex Tudor's career. On the back of hundreds of injuries to Surrey's senior bowlers, Tudor got his chance at Lord's and impressed with his pace and bounce. He could also swing the ball away in his early days. However, Tudor became the great enigma of English cricket. When fit he was a real handful and a massive asset to any side. That was the problem though; people grew frustrated with him not being fit for enough games. The truth was that his body wasn't strong enough in the right areas to cope with bowling fast on a daily basis. We used to joke with him in the gym that he only ever seemed to work on his 'beach muscles' and neglect his legs and core area. Never once did Tudor take 50 wickets in a season, although he did play a big part in our Championship-winning years. Tudor should have gone on to take 200 Test wickets instead of the injury-littered career he had.

The season lurched on; with no sign of silverware once more the club was getting restless. Clinton and Edwards were surely going to be replaced. The atmosphere in the camp wasn't crash hot either. The words 'team spirit' get bandied about a lot when it comes to team sports. The facts of the matter are that if you are playing in a winning side the team spirit is always good. You are winning and everyone is happy. Play in a side that wins nothing, underachieves, and where players are in and out of the side because of a lack of form, and then try and tell me the team spirit is good.

We did have a good group of players though, and as we were all of an age to go out and enjoy ourselves we didn't let ourselves down in that area. Saturday nights normally meant putting your best clothes on and not coming home until the early hours of the next morning. A game in Derby was a case in point. Around 2am, kicking out time, there was no sign of our overseas player Carl Rackemann. Not being in the greatest of health myself I wasn't in the mood to look for him. But find him we did, lying down on the pavement virtually unconscious. 'Hammered' would be a good description of how we found him. Trying to get him back on his feet would be another issue. Weighing in at nearly 18 stone, Rackemann was a big unit. Quite how we lifted him and got him into a cab I shall never know. We got him to bed though. How he was going to play cricket was another matter. Come next morning and there was no sign of him anywhere. He eventually arrived at the ground during warm-ups and loosened up in dark glasses. Once on the field and bowling, he delivered what can only be described as utter garbage. He was still drunk, 12 hours on.

On another trip, this time in Worcester, Rackemann was celebrating his birthday and was looking for some celebratory 'action'. After trawling the bars of Worcester and with no sign of anything happening, the big fella took himself off home, a little disgruntled. As he got back to the hotel he found two girls standing outside having a chat, bemoaning the fact they couldn't get a drink. Cue Rackemann's birthday celebrations – back to his room and more company than he bargained for. We got Rackemann at the end of his career and Surrey didn't see the best of him. He was a top man though and great to have in the dressing room.

I managed to get fit again by mid-August and put together a good run in the side. I also bowled really well and got a lot of wickets. Adam had now assumed the captaincy role on a permanent basis when Alec was away. I was happy to be playing cricket again after the nightmare of the previous two years. I had managed just 16 games in two years; I missed exactly half the Championship fixtures in that time and it would take forever to shake off the tag of always being injured. Injuries and frustration had brought out the worst in me; I even had a semi fight in the dressing room with one of my best mates, Nadeem Shahid. I didn't like the person I had become. I was lazy and selfish and a liability for the club. I had to grow up.

Eventually I came through the other side, learnt a lot about myself and hopefully improved as a person. I got married to Loraine in September, Ellie was nearly six months old and I am sure this helped me calm down. Good times were just around the corner for me and the club.

Me, Mum and Darren

Darren and me

School photo

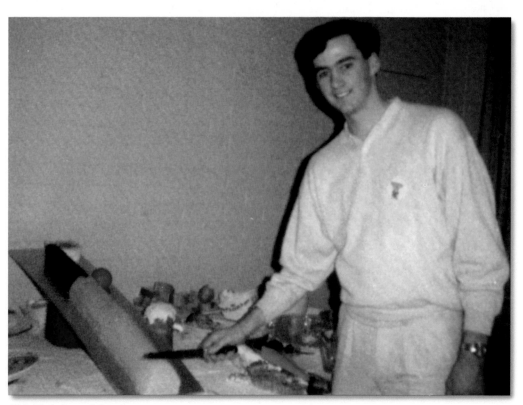

18th Birthday celebrations

Bowling at The Oval in 1985

I'm third from right in this Youth World Cup squad, 1987

Group shot, Zimbabwe A Tour, 1990

Preparing to bat, Zimbabwe A Tour, 1990

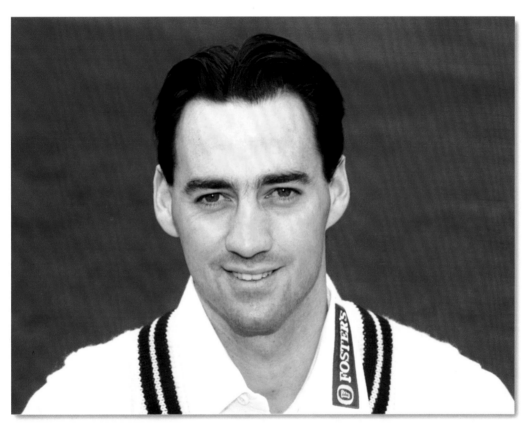

Official Surrey photocall, 1996

On tour

Skiing

Taking the wicket of Matthew Maynard (Glamorgan Dragons) for Surrey Lions, 1999

Celebrating Surrey's win over Lancashire in the PPP Healthcare County Championship match played at Old Trafford, 2000

Examining the selection of used balls with umpire John Steele, after he asked for a ball change in a Surrey match against Essex, 2001

Playing for England, taking the wicket of Graeme Smith of South Africa, 2003

Some of my Cricket moments playing for England against South Africa in 2003

With my daughters Charlotte and Ellie

Thommo Foxy and me... best mates

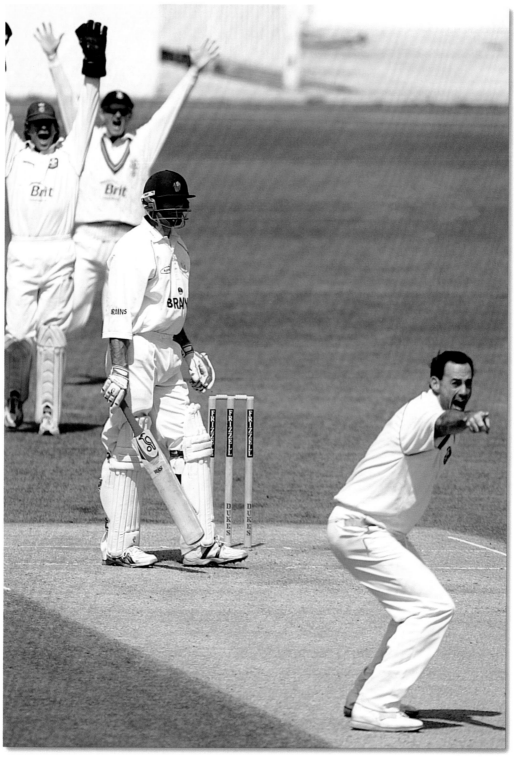

Appealing for the wicket of David Hemp of Glamorgan in a Surrey match, The Oval 2005

Official Surrey photocall, 2006

# Success At Last

After the nightmare, in terms of both performance and management in 1994 and 1995, the club looked in a new direction. Vic Dodds, the cricket chairman at the time, had a very good relationship with David Gilbert. Gilbert had played fleetingly for Australia but in recent times had brought the Australian 'A' team to England and earned very good reviews with his handling of the side. Surrey were in desperate need of a change of direction and Gilbert was given the job of turning around a talented, but underachieving team.

New players came into the club. Chris Lewis and Brendon Julian would give us great options in the one-day game as well as more fire power in the longer form of the game. In addition to those two, the club would have another bonus in the return to form and fitness of one of their long-term players – me. The nightmare that had been '94 and '95 had well and truly gone. I was fit and hungry and keen to impress the new management.

Coming from the outside Gilbert had no preconceived ideas on how Surrey operated and effectively had a blank piece of paper to work from. Unlike Steve Rixon who came in later on, Gilbert took time to assess his players and work out how to get the best of them. One of the first things he did was 'knock down the wall'. The club had always operated a 'capped' players dressing room and a 'non-capped' players dressing room. It was seen as an incentive to get your 'cap' and make the transition from one dressing room to the next, which was seen as the ultimate honour. It was a 'class' system, a system that Gilbert couldn't understand and wanted to get rid of. His idea was that if you play in the same team you should all be equals. Not changing in separate dressing rooms. The wall went and we were one big dressing room. Equality was what it was all about. No longer did the batsmen stroll into the nets first, the bowlers batted first on some practice days. Everyone was made to feel as important as everyone else.

It wasn't all about cricket either. We went to The Belfry for a pre-season get together; no cricket, but a bit of training and team bonding. One of the things we did was play golf. We split into fours and everyone had to play. We had guys who had never picked up a golf club before playing on the Ryder Cup course! It was all part of the 'do everything together' policy that would encapsulate Gilbert's reign. In my fourball we had a couple of golfers, one guy who had played once or twice and Joey Benjamin. We played a 'Texas Scramble' format. This meant if you weren't much of a player it didn't really matter in this team event. On the first tee we all hit off and Benjamin was last to hit, barely making contact with the ball with a swing more reminiscent of someone chopping wood. However, the fun and games did not end there. On the green we got Benji to putt first. Now, clearly Benji had never seen anyone play golf before, because that would explain his Tiger Woods-style full swing with a putter. Luckily we stopped him before he made contact with the ball and luckily we didn't get thrown off the course. Benji was a great character. Coming from Warwickshire he turned himself into an England player with his nippy away swingers and was a great addition to our staff. However, you could write another book on his off-field exploits, and they mainly concerned his driving ability. Arriving in London, Benji was given a sponsored car. The garage we were collecting our cars from was just around the corner from the ground. We all walked around and drove our cars back, except Benji. He got someone else to collect his car. In fact he didn't use his car much at all. His girlfriend used to come down on the weekend and use it; it was all getting a bit suspicious. After a while we had to do a bit of investigating and in the glove compartment of his car we found his 'L' plates. Benji couldn't even drive, yet he had a club car. Priceless. Once he got his licence and his club car back, the fun started again – mainly watching him park or trying to use his mobile phone while driving.

Back in the camp you could sense a change in the squad. We were now quite experienced with a fair share of current internationals in Thorpe, Stewart and Lewis. We had good squad players in Jason Ratcliffe and Nadeem Shahid – two guys who knew they weren't first-choice players but would come into the team when Stewart and Thorpe were away with the England team. The importance of players like this would have a major role in our success over the next few years. We felt ready to compete in all four competitions, but without a recognised quality spinner the one-day competitions would represent our strongest chance of winning some silverware.

We had a bit of a stuttering start, lost the first Sunday League game down at Somerset, reached the quarter-finals of the Benson and Hedges and took a while to record our first win in the Championship. After the mauling Yorkshire gave us at The Oval in the quarter-final of the Benson and Hedges, we found some form. You could sense a team coming together. Adam Hollioake was having more of an influence as captain of the side when Alec Stewart was away on England duty, and he and Gilbert worked well together. I always felt that Alec wasn't entirely comfortable with David Gilbert. Maybe it was the England v Australia thing or it may have been that Gilbert and Hollioake, both Aussies by birth, were on a better wavelength when it came to cricket-related matters. Adam was growing as a leader and Alec felt this too and would stand down at the end of the season. It must have been so difficult to play for your country every other week and in between come back to a side that was responding better to a new leader. It didn't make it easy for the team either. To have players in and out of the side, England players coming back from international duty, tired, and in need of a rest, didn't help the flow of the season. In time we would cope better and deal with regular team changes, but this season our squad probably still wasn't strong enough.

One of the stand out games from the first half of the season came in the Sunday League game at home to Leicestershire. On a very good pitch, in perfect batting conditions, we bowled them out for 48 in just 22 overs. In reply we knocked off the runs in just 4.3 overs! It was a bizarre day; the game started at 2pm and was all over by 3.45pm. Celebratory team drinks on the King's Road were the order of the day.

Enjoyment and team bonding were very much on the agenda in Gilbert's time at the club. Every Saturday night on away trips meant team night out. Sunday games started at 2pm then and with a lie in on the Sunday morning it meant only one thing on Saturday night – party time. Most coaches would actively discourage drinking and late nights but

# BICKERS

Gilbert encouraged it. In fact if you got to bed earlier than he did you were considered a bit soft. It's not the sort of thing you could get away with now in the era of dieticians and lifestyle coaches. But back then it had a very positive effect on our team and brought us closer together.

Our last defeat in the Sunday League came on 21st July against Sussex at Guildford. An incredible 117 from Martin Speight took the game away from us. It wasn't all bad news that day; later that night Charlotte would become our second daughter. I spent the next day with her lying on top of me trying to catch up on some lost sleep. With six games of the season to go we knew we couldn't afford any more slip ups. Gradually we covered the six games with few alarms. Two home games against potential challengers and a tricky away game at Cardiff would decide our season. The first of these games, against Warwickshire, we bowled well to restrict them to 185. A stuttering chase saw us win the game by two wickets; nerves were starting to get the better of us. Did we know how to win? Did we know how to close the door and seal the deal? It had been 14 long years since the club had last won a trophy and the pressure was starting to tell. The second of these games, against Northants would be our toughest test yet.

They were still very much in the hunt to win the league and had a formidable team, with Curtley Ambrose the star performer. However, it was David Capel with a brilliant hundred who took them to a big score of 237 in 40 overs. We had even more work to do at 100-5 with time running out. Enter Nadeem Shahid and Chris Lewis, and out of the crisis we were in, emerged a glimmer of light. When that partnership broke it was still very 50/50 and when I got to the wicket we needed seven an over and it was not looking too clever. With good running and the occasional big shot we got it down to six runs required off the last over which was to be bowled by Kevin Curran. Lewis got out at the start of the over and once again it was in the balance. Richard Pearson joined me and after a couple of scrambled singles it was down to two to win off the last ball and I'm facing up, shaking like a leaf. The crowd was big for a Sunday, the noise was immense and you could cut the atmosphere with a knife. As Curran ran in to bowl that final ball, our season rested on the outcome. We were challenging in the Championship but had left a lot to do to win the league and it would eventually prove too much. Years of underachievement would carry on if we lost this game and I was in bloody control of the outcome. I knew he would try and bowl a yorker and I knew I was going to try and hit the ball down the ground and scramble two runs. The ball fell right in the slot and I smashed it for all I was worth through wide long on for four. Cue pandemonium. I sprinted off the field as people ran on; I couldn't wait to get into the dressing room to celebrate. And we hadn't even won the league yet. One more game to go; win and we are Champions.

That Sunday in Cardiff in early September will live long in the memory. Followed there by thousands of long-suffering Surrey supporters, we finally got over the finishing line. In truth Glamorgan didn't put up that much of a fight, but we didn't care. We were professional in our performance and a season of hard work was finally rewarded.

Batting first, Glamorgan never got going, losing regular wickets and posting just 159 – a score that never looked like being enough once Alistair Brown had taken to Otis Gibson. It was left to Nadeem Shahid, one of the unsung heroes of the team, to hit the winning runs with eight overs remaining. The relief was palpable, and we sure celebrated that night. We did have the small matter of a Championship match the next day to play, and I am sure a few of us were still over the alcohol limit as we took the field at 11am. Our Championship challenge fizzled out in Cardiff, but a trophy was what we came to Wales for, and we took one home.

Adam Hollioake had not only led the team well in Alec's absence, but also established himself as the premier one-day bowler in the country. Thirty-nine wickets at 12 runs apiece broke the record for wickets taken. I came second with 21 wickets and more importantly, had played every game that season. After the two previous years where I was becoming a liability, it was great to play such a part in the season. I ended up with 66 wickets in the Championship too and in the process established myself back in the side and would start a run of great success in Surrey colours.

As so often happens in life, a good thing happens and then life has a way of knocking you back down again. Graham Kersey, our wicket-keeper, was involved in a car crash in Brisbane on Christmas Eve. We were all informed he was in a bad way, in a coma with serious injuries. It was like someone had driven a knife straight through your heart. Kersey was probably the most popular man on our staff. A Kent boy, he had come to Surrey and established himself as one of the rising stars in the game. He was just a great lad, full of energy, with a desire to be the best. He made us tick behind the stumps, always encouraging, always positive. His injuries were too severe; he died in hospital on New Year's Day aged 25. It was a painful lesson on how cruel life can be. His parents never recovered, his Father died not long after his accident from what relatives described as a broken heart. I read at the service for Graham to a large gathering of people. I barely held it together long enough to complete my reading. Afterwards I sat in the church and cried and cried. I hoped it would be the last time I had to go through something like that again for a very long time. Sadly it wasn't.

Winning the Sunday League merely whetted our appetite for more honours. At the start of the 1997 season we strengthened our team with the addition of Ian Salisbury from Sussex. Sals had been in and around the England team and was going to play a major part in completing ours. We had sorely lacked a match-winning spinner; Richard Pearson had done a really good job in our one-day team but didn't have the variety a leg spinner would bring. Jon Batty had the unenviable job of replacing Kersey behind the stumps. We started the season without an overseas player, but after a slowish start we were alerted to someone who would have the biggest influence in my time at the club: Saqlain Mushtaq.

The 1997 season was also my Benefit Year. It all kicked off with a trip to Jersey at the request of my chairman, Richard Thompson. His club side used to take part in this six a side tournament in March, and he got me to take part on the basis I could run an auction over the weekend and make a bit of money. We took a strong side; my brother came, David Ward and Ali Brown too. The rest of the side was made up of a couple of mates who were there as drinkers rather than cricketers. It was a fairly riotous weekend. The tradition was you didn't sleep at all on the first night, but you drank and played cards, then straight on to the cricket tournament in the morning. We did scrape a bit of money together on the auction but nothing like what Darren earned at the card game on the last night. Not being the biggest gambler in the world Darren was always a bit cautious when it came to playing with the big players. However he got on a bit of a run as dealer at Blackjack and before he knew it he was up a couple of thousand pounds. The money changing hands was staggering. People were writing their own bank notes and IOUs were all over the place. When the games came to an end Darren had enough money to buy a new kitchen. I don't think he bothered playing again.

With the weather playing a huge part in our slow start in the Championship, the Benson and Hedges became our prime focus. We had some new ideas. Ben Hollioake, was starting to make a bit of a name for himself and was elevated to number three. Batting flexibility was the watchword. An early defeat to Kent in the group stage meant the game at Gloucester was a massive one for us. A score of 280 is normally enough for the home team batting first, but in Alistair Brown and Ben Hollioake we had two match winners of the highest calibre. And so it proved. We were on our way. Wins over Hampshire, Sussex and the British Universities took us to the quarter-finals and a match with Essex at Chelmsford. Essex were a strong side. A line-up of Prichard, Gooch, Law, Hussain and Irani were a match for any team in the country. Personally I was very nervous. A great batting wicket normally meant lots of runs and especially against that line-up. However, someone was looking after me that day as I removed Hussain and Law cheaply and in doing so won the Man of the Match award for my 3-40 off 10 overs. We restricted Essex to just 214 and ran out comfortable winners by six wickets with eight overs to spare. It was a great performance, possibly one of the best performances I had played in to that point.

The semi-final draw gave us Leicestershire at home and we had a new addition to the side in Saqlain Mushtaq. Saqi had come out of obscurity. No one had really seen him bowl and there was even a rumour going around that he could spin the ball the other way with an off-spinner's action. We would see plenty of that over the next few years. We knew he was good though. In the nets he would go through the full repertoire, bamboozling all our batters and giving us an insight into what opposition batters would be facing in the coming years.

Leicestershire won the toss and elected to bowl on a belting wicket. We lost Brown and Hollioake early, but in Stewart and Thorpe we had two proven performers at the highest level. They gave a batting master class with 87 and 79 respectively. With Adam Hollioake smashing a quick-fire 63 we amassed 308 off our 50 overs – a huge score. In reply Leicestershire collapsed. Another dominating performance, and another Man of the Match award for me. I took the first four wickets and Leicestershire were crushed by 130 runs. Saqlain was barely needed, although his time would come.

After all the semi-final defeats in recent years this was another step towards Surrey becoming a big force in the game. Too many times we had been guilty of underperforming in the big games and letting the pressure get to us. But the tide was turning. We now had big match players, guys who were used to playing in front of big crowds. It is so important as a sportsman to enjoy the big occasions, and now I felt we looked forward to the big games. The final was something we had targeted and now we were there. But blocking our path was Kent, probably the best one-day side in the country and one hell of a challenge.

Lord's finals are huge affairs. People say it's a great day out. It's only a great day out if you win the game. After playing in a losing final against

# BICKERS

Hampshire I can tell you, that was one day out I didn't much enjoy. I wanted to walk away from that ground with the big Benson and Hedges Gold trophy in my hands. I wanted to smoke a big cigar on the Lord's dressing room balcony with a glass of champagne in the other hand.

We prepared well. By this stage of the season we had a very established side in this competition and a game plan that didn't need much discussion. We did talk a lot about Kent though and worked out good plans for their batters. They were very powerful and we would need to be at the top of our game. I was nervous as hell come the morning of the match. In truth the game had been on my mind for the previous two weeks. The usual thoughts of messing up on the big stage were on my mind and I wanted the game over and done with so I could get a good night's sleep.

We won the toss and bowled. After a loose first over I got lucky and Matt Walker dragged a wide back on his stumps. With Chris Lewis removing the dangerous Mathew Fleming we were in the box seat early. It got better for us as I nipped a ball back into Allan Wells' pads and he was gone too – 23-3 and Kent were struggling badly. Even the normally belligerent Trevor Ward was subdued as the scoring rate limped along. A hint of resistance from Nigel Llong and Mark Ealham was snuffed out by Saqlain, and Lewis returned with perfect timing to remove the dangerous Graham Cowdrey. A score of 212 in 50 overs looked below par. The sun was out, the pitch a belter and even the early loss of Alistair Brown wasn't going to dampen our day.

When Ben Hollioake entered the arena no one knew we were about to witness one of the great Lord's final innings. We knew Ben was talented but this was something else. He hardly broke sweat compiling a scintillating 98 off 112 balls and with Alec the other end guiding him through it, the result was never in doubt. We had dominated the game from the first over and ran out easy winners. Two trophies in two years proved the Sunday League win wasn't just a one off. We had come to Lord's and beaten the best one-day side in the country and in doing so shifted the power in the game. We were ready for more.

The Championship was just a damp squib for us in 1997 as we finished in eighth position. We did get going in the second half of the season. Saqlain was proving a great signing. Ten wickets against Durham at The Oval, followed by another 10 wickets at Lord's including a hat-trick. Quite simply he was a magician. Not only was he a genius, he was possibly the nicest guy you could ever meet. We had a heart to heart team meeting during the '97 season and views were aired, good and bad about all your team-mates. It was to get all your thoughts out in the middle and listen to what other people had to say about you both as a person, and a player. We all had our say and there were some pretty disparaging things said about some people in that room. But every time it was Saqi's turn to speak he couldn't find anything even mildly wrong to say about anybody.

Saqi had international commitments that meant we didn't see a lot of him. He did leave his mark though. Thirty-two wickets at 19 apiece, he created quite an impression. We had no hesitation in signing him long term. Sals was injured for most of the season and we couldn't get them on the pitch together, but we knew we had the makings of a Championship-winning team. We had struggled to bowl sides out twice at The Oval relying on seam bowling. We had to base our side around our two spinners, with support from our other seamers. We knew we had a batting side that would score enough runs, but taking 20 wickets in a game was proving too difficult. We had tried with Waqar Younis and it was beyond even him. The county game in this country is so difficult for quick bowlers and a shift in thinking was required. Spin would be the answer. We felt '98 would be our year.

I had another good year, 44 wickets at 26 apiece and 300 runs in the Championship. And for the first time the players' 'Player of the Year' award. This award meant so much to me. I only missed one Championship game for the second year in a row and was finally getting the 'always injured' tag off my back. The players' 'Player of the Year' award was the first of five in a row, something I am immensely proud of. To be accepted by your peers as the most valuable player in your team is the ultimate accolade. It became a good habit.

Before the start of the 1998 season there was important family business to attend to. After 28 years it was time finally to meet my Father. It had been on my mind for a long time. I knew it was something that I had to do. We had finally made contact after one of Loraine's cousins met him in his taxi cab in the Lake District. We knew he lived in that area as there had been a couple of sightings of him in the past. Loraine managed to track down the company he worked for and got an address for him. I wrote a letter and sent it off, not knowing if I would ever get a reply. When I did, I knew it was only a matter of time before we met. Darren was initially reluctant but we talked about it and came to the conclusion if we didn't make the effort it would be an opportunity missed.

We arranged to meet him in Oxendale, just outside Windermere. The train journey up was edgy and nervous. We didn't know this man at all. He came across well in his letter but meeting him would be a different kettle of fish. We got off the train, and in the distance coming towards us was our Dad, instantly recognisable and bearing a striking resemblance to how Darren will look in 20 years. It was all a bit bizarre, but at the same time it felt quite natural. We all hit it off well, went for a meal and got to know each other a little. It wasn't time for searching questions so we talked about cricket, football and golf; passions we all shared. He said he hadn't wanted to come back into our lives after we had become famous because it would send us the wrong message, so he had to wait for us to contact him. We stayed up for the weekend, met his friends, had quite a few beers and enjoyed ourselves. It was clear how proud he was of us both. His friends spoke in glowing terms about him and we both saw a lovely kind-hearted man. It was the right thing to do and we are both glad we did it. We see each other a couple of times a year now. There are still 300 miles between us, but fortunately not 28 years.

For the 1998 season we lost Chris Lewis who went back to Leicester after a couple of interesting years in London. Lewis was for the most part fascinating entertainment. Would he arrive at the right time? Would he be wearing the right kit? And what crazy thing would he do today? He was good value in our team and we would miss him in one-day cricket.

Saqlain was back, and available for most of the year. His partnership with Ian Salisbury was exciting and Alex Tudor was making a name for himself also. We had all the ingredients to mount a challenge and it was becoming very important to win the Championship soon. The players were reaching their peak and it was the title we all wanted.

# BICKERS

We were in the running for so long that season. The game at Cheltenham against Gloucestershire was to be the crucial match for us. We won the toss on a good but fast wicket. Courtney Walsh was Gloucestershire's main weapon and he came at us hard. A brilliant hundred by Adam Hollioake took us to a great total of 297 and in return we bowled them out for 167. I was at the top of my game and took 5-34. A lead of 130 should have won us the game but with Walsh in hostile form we were bowled out for just 135. We just couldn't deal with the pace and bounce of Walsh. He was a phenomenal performer and you could only admire the way he kept running in hard.

It left Gloucester to chase 265; we knew it would go down to the wire. Gloucester got to 44 before they lost their first wicket. However, an incident involving Saqlain will stick in my mind as long as I live. Tim Hancock tried to slog sweep Saqi over mid wicket but only succeeded in hitting the ball high in the air in the vicinity of our little spinner. In what felt like an eternity for the ball to come back down to the ground, Saqi had positioned himself near the stumps at the bowler's end. The non striker had wandered down the pitch to end up next to the batter who, thinking he was going to be caught, just stood in his crease. If you can imagine Saqi standing there waiting for the ball to come out of the sky and then the ball landing five yards away from where he was positioned you would have a fair idea of what was going to happen next. With both batsmen down by the keeper, Saqi, on missing the catch, gets the ball and instead of walking casually up to the stumps at the non striker's end to remove the bails, hurls the ball to the keeper's end. At this point the non striker thinks he has got a chance if he runs back to the bowler's end. Jon Batty gets the ball and hurls it back to Saqi who fumbles it, scrambles around in the dust trying to pick the damn thing up, eventually does so and knocks the bails off. With all this commotion going on, the batter makes his ground. No run out, no wicket, but fielders creased up in laughter. It was such an important moment in the game but you could not help yourself laughing and it summed Saqi up beautifully. An incredible bowler... but as a fielder? Don't put your mortgage on him holding a catch.

A regular fall of wickets saw us get right back in the game and with Gloucester 160-6 the game should have been ours. Saqi was bowling beautifully. I had another three wickets, but was operating on near empty I was that tired. Martyn Ball came in and played an extraordinary innings of 48 not out to guide them home. He hit the ball everywhere we didn't have a fielder. A dropped catch by Nadeem Shahid on the deep square boundary summed up our day, when they still needed 20 to win with two wickets in hand. It was a hammer blow to our title ambitions.

We also lost to Yorkshire at Headingley on one of the greenest wickets I have ever seen. In their attempts to nullify Saqi and Sals we played on a damp green wicket in August. It wouldn't be the last time Yorkshire used underhand tactics against us either. A win at Durham gave us a glimmer of hope going into the last game of the season at home to Leicestershire.

If we won the game and limited Leicester to just a few bonus points we could win the league. If we lost and results went against us, we would finish fifth and out of the prize money. So, guess where we finished? Fifth. We lost Saqi to international commitments – a major blow. Leicester had played great cricket all year and were flying. We had them 100-4 at lunch, but when I succumbed to injury shortly after lunch the wheels came off.

# BICKERS

Ben Smith with a double hundred, and hundreds from Habib and Nixon put the game out of reach. We finally got a bat shortly before the close of day two and ended the day on 8-4, wheels now firmly off. Defeat followed and the season ended without a trophy. It was a bitter pill to swallow. We lost to all the teams that finished above us and to be fair hadn't done enough to win the Championship. We learnt valuable lessons. We had to adapt better to conditions that didn't suit our batsmen. And we had to become more ruthless in the pursuit of victory.

In one-day cricket we were poor, finishing bottom of the Sunday League and crashing out to Lancashire in the quarter-finals of the Benson and Hedges, and in the quarters of the Nat West to Derby.

I had another great year, didn't miss a single game in the Championship, but still not a sniff of an England call. Sixty-five wickets at 20 and 433 runs in the Championship. I was approaching the peak of my career. Years of self doubt were behind me; I was confident and respected by my team-mates and the opposition. But I was hungry for more. The Championship was the prize we were all so desperate to win. We didn't have to wait too much longer.

# Martin Bicknell

# The Long Wait is Over

Although we always thought 1999 was going to be our chance to win the Championship, there were still many obstacles to overcome. There was the World Cup, held in England, that would rob us of some key players. Saqlain, whom many people thought was key to our chances, would not be available for the first eight games of the Championship season. And we had to take more wickets from other sources to win enough games.

The squad was pretty much established, although we did have Darren Bicknell coming back from a season out through back injury, to bolster the batting. Ian Ward had been a great re-signing for us and was to have a great year. He, along with Mark Butcher – temporarily out of the England reckoning – would create a great opening partnership. Alex Tudor, free from injury, would be a great foil for me, and Ian Salisbury really stepped up.

We were lucky to have Adam Hollioake. Adam was in the World Cup squad but due to his lack of opportunities he was allowed to come and play for us. Adam was turning into a great captain. He was a great leader of people and someone you would go through fire and water for. He'd never been taught the meaning of 'throw in the towel'. In any situation he could only see victory, long after the rest of us were thinking ahead to the journey home. He knew when to wind things up a bit too. If we were just cruising, or needed firing up he would normally have the solution. Our warm-ups always included a game of football. Once, in the middle of a four-day game that had started to drift, Adam sensed an opportunity to stir things up. Mark Butcher was dawdling on the ball and in true Hollioake footballing tradition, Adam came straight through the back of him. All hell broke loose, a full scale argument developed between Butch and Adam and before we knew it we were all involved. It sure got us going. Job done for the day.

With his Australian background Adam loved the physicality of sport. One of his passions is boxing, and he would often try to get the boys involved in his sparring sessions. Alex Tudor, with an uncanny resemblance to Frank Bruno, fancied his chances. With Adam under strict instructions not to hit Tudor in the head, the sparring was going along nicely. But Tudor, thinking he now has the measure of Adam starts aiming in a few head shots. Hollioake, starting to get a little irritated by Tudor's antics, decides enough is enough and an upper cut to Bruno's jaw sends him crashing to the floor. The fight took place just before a team meeting. We all assembled and Tudor came into the room last. Well, if it wasn't Bambi on ice. It was all we could do to stop ourselves collapsing into fits of laughter. Sparring was banned shortly after.

There was another time when Adam's boxing skills came into good use. We were on an end of season jaunt to Guernsey to play in a 'charity' match against Leicestershire, and get drunk. Adam and Butch decided on a 24-hour 'drinkathon'. Unfortunately the game was scheduled for part of the 24 hours. Butch, having moved himself down the order to 10 was required to bat to win the game and his last wicket partner was me, also suitably inebriated. We put on 30 and were only a few runs short of our target. I pushed a ball through the covers and set off for a run. However, there was a problem. Butch had fallen asleep at the non striker's end, literally. We managed to wake him eventually and we won the game with an unlikely 40-run partnership. The evening carried on as the day had started. I looked round at one point and saw Adam asleep standing up against the wall in the night club. Nadeem Shahid was having fun with the locals, trying to chat up one of their girlfriends. Visibly upset, the locals had a pop at Nad and drew blood. At this point I could see it all about to kick off. I was preparing myself for the ensuing brawl when Adam brushed past me. He had the scent of violence in his nostrils and walked straight up to this guy and lamped him smack in the face. The 'local' didn't get up. Adam disappeared as quickly as he had arrived and normal service resumed. If you ever fancy a fight, Adam is your man.

And then there was Medders. Keith Medlycott had stepped up from 2nd XI duty at the start of the 1998 season when David Gilbert had left to take up a job at Sussex. Hollioake and Medlycott were the perfect foil. Hollioake was all bravado and leadership and Medlycott was the background man, ensuring things were running smoothly. He was an excellent man manager and his success in South Africa had taught him how to win. A bit of a larrikin in his youth, he knew when to let players enjoy themselves and he knew when to rein them back in.

The season started off a little slowly. April can be a problem for creating momentum and you can find yourself a couple of wins behind early on if your games are affected by rain. After two drawn games we found ourselves at Northampton in need of a win. The pitch was hard and fast, and in Devon Malcolm, Northants had the perfect fast bowler. After losing the toss we bowled very well to restrict them to 248 all out. In reply we lost a wicket early and then Malcolm broke Nadeem Shahid's arm with a rapid bouncer. Nad was an exceptional player against quick bowling and a key man in our team. His was a severe loss. Adam played a gutsy innings but was running out of partners near the end of the innings. At nine down Nad courageously came out to try and get him to three figures, but unfortunately Adam ran himself out for 96 trying to get back on strike.

We got up to 286 and the game was very much 50/50. Alex Tudor then bowled beautifully, getting 5-64, and I chipped in with my second four-wicket haul of the match. But Northants had got to 338, a lead of 300. It was going to be a tough chase with only 10 batsmen, and Devon Malcolm in full flow. It would take an innings of high class from Graham Thorpe of 138 not out to see us home. Suddenly we were off and running.

Another win in the next game against Essex confirmed our belief that this really could be our year. Chasing a tricky 270 in the last innings of the game would often have been beyond us, but now we had players who knew how to get the job done. It was Ali Brown this time. A superb innings of 110 not out showed what an excellent player he had become. Brown had burst onto the scene in the mid-Nineties with three hundreds in 70, 71 and 79 balls – and this was in first-class cricket, not in the one-day game. With this mature innings against Essex he showed he wasn't just a cultured slogger but had a great cricket brain and knew the way to win a game of cricket. He would do it again at Swansea later in the year to win that game too.

We were winning tight games. It wasn't all about rolling over sides and winning comfortably. The Somerset game at The Oval became our third win in a row and took us to the top of the table. On a typical flat Oval wicket we had dominated the game. Hundreds from Denz (the nickname for Darren came about after the cricket chairman at the time, Derek Newton, thought that was his name) and Salisbury, put us in a dominant position. We were having a real struggle to bowl them out for a second time, but with about half an hour left we got the last wicket. We were left with 48 to score off five overs in near darkness. Jason Ratcliffe played a great little cameo of 22 to win the game for us. Andrew Caddick could have run up, bowled a few bouncers and some down the leg side to prevent us from scoring the runs, but he tried to take wickets. We all thought he must have been on a bonus for wickets taken; either that or he just wasn't being very clever. He helped us win the match.

Jason Ratcliffe epitomised the Surrey staff that year. Not a first-choice player by any means, but a great squad man. If the England players were available, Ratters didn't play. Instead he would have to go off and play second-team cricket. He didn't complain, he just got on with it. We have youngsters at Surrey now who throw in the towel if they are asked to go and play second-team cricket. Take Nayan Doshi for example. He's a good bowler, not a great one, but someone who has done well in patches for the first team. In 2007, after being left out of the first team, he handed in his notice. All players' careers go through dips in form and you may find yourself in and out of the side. But it says an awful lot about you, both as a player and a person, if you walk away from the challenge. If they don't want to be part of a squad, get rid of them. They are not team players. The culture we have today is one where players expect instant success or they'll go and try and get it somewhere else. It's not that simple.

# BICKERS

Sometimes you have to bide your time, learn your trade and make the most of the opportunity if it comes along.

Ratcliffe produced a spell at Tunbridge Wells against Kent that went a long way towards us winning that match. With Kent getting back into the game and no one really fancying bowling into the strong wind at one end, Adam threw the ball to part-time bowler Ratcliffe, who took three wickets including the key wicket of Andrew Symonds. Now it's fair to say that I didn't ever get along with Symonds so this wicket gave me considerable pleasure and we let him know. A couple of years prior to this game we had been playing Gloucester at Cheltenham College. Symonds in his brash, arrogant way was trying to provoke me, verbally and with his bat. He had already hit me back over my head for six and was looking for more of the same. I bowled a ball just back of a length and he defended it straight back down the ground.

I picked it up and looked at him, waiting for him to say something. He didn't disappoint. 'If you bowl it there again I am going to hit you over that tent' he said, looking at a tent over deep mid wicket. "Game on" I thought. I ran up and bowled it in the same place; he took on the shot but only managed to top edge it straight up in the air into the waiting hands of Jon Batty behind the stumps. By now, with all the banter that had been going on, the whole team had gathered around Symonds and he got the biggest send off he had ever received. It was a lovely moment; we don't get on, me and Symonds.

The season had reached half way. We had drawn with last year's champions, Leicestershire, and now had Lancashire, Muralitharan and Flintoff to deal with. I missed the game through illness. With Saqi still away injured, we had our work cut out to take 20 wickets. But that was the thing about this season – there was always someone else to step up and take the lead role. In this game Alex Tudor took eight wickets and Mark Butcher, with his occasional seamers, took 4-30 in the second innings to leave us chasing 160. Against Murali this was not going to be an easy chase but we scraped over the line by four wickets. On the last morning I followed the game on Ceefax and ticked off every run we needed. It was getting really tense now. We were playing some great cricket and winning all the tight games – surely this was going to be our year?

Saqi was back. He destroyed Durham at The Oval with 12 wickets in the game. They had no answer to his genius. Saqi only played seven games in 1999, but he took 58 wickets at 11 a piece, a truly phenomenal achievement. He was unplayable. We went to Hove in August and were confronted by a damp green wicket. We lost the toss and were in all sorts of trouble at 55-6 before I helped Adam out with a timely half century and we got up to 224. Overnight, Sussex were 100-2. We had a team meeting before the start of the next day's play and hoped to bowl them out for around 250. Thanks to the little maestro we did better than that. On a pitch offering virtually no assistance, Saqi took 7-19 including a hat-trick. From 100-2 Sussex were bowled out for 115. With Sussex in a state of shock we blitzed them with the bat, Denz scoring his last hundred for the club. With his back injury and then the arrival of Ian Ward he wasn't playing in all the games and virtually not at all in one-day cricket. At the end of the season he would move to Nottinghamshire. At tea time, after scoring the hundred, I could see what it meant to him. There was a certain chemistry between us. I knew exactly what was going on in his head and he knew I knew. The second innings was a formality. Another four wickets for Saqi and the title was within our grasp.

The trip to Derby followed – never the nicest place to play cricket— but we had a job to do. Sky covered the game and Botham rambled on in his commentary about Saqi being the main reason we were winning the league. I felt a bit gutted not to get a mention. It was by no means a one-man show. To win a title it takes team effort. There was probably more drama off the field than on it. On the journey to the ground I was following Mark Butcher when he took off down the M1. I was pretty sure I was going the right way to the ground but when I arrived there was no sight of him. Medders confirmed that Butch had had to go home for personal reasons. His marriage to Alec's sister Judy had gone pear-shaped and he had to deal with matters. Although it weakened our side, Ian Ward's first hundred for the club ensured we got to 350. In reply Derby couldn't deal with a rampant Surrey attack. An innings victory and another seven wickets in the game for me. I hoped Botham left the ground with a slightly different opinion. We were so close now. Only Notts at The Oval to come; a win there and it was ours.

At the back end of the Derby game I pulled a calf muscle and would miss the biggest game of the season. There were in fact still three games to go so we knew it was only a matter of time, but we wanted to win the title at The Oval in front of a big crowd. Excitement was growing at the club. It had been 28 years since the last Championship triumph and the natives were getting restless. We put out a very inexperienced seam bowling line-up due to injury. No Bicknell, Tudor or Ben Hollioake, but the young lads who came in did a fine job. With Saqi and Sals pulling the strings it was all over inside two days. The only question was would we complete the job on the second night? Chasing 150 in 25 overs it was left to Ian Ward to smash the ball down the ground with a couple of overs left to seal the deal. It was over, the champagne corks flew into the air and we were Champions at last. Even though I hadn't played in the game I was physically exhausted watching.

After 15 games of the season we had won 12 and drawn three. We would go on to draw the last two games of the year to give us an unbeaten season. We won the league by a staggering 55 points. The squad had all contributed. Everyone had played a part and all the planning and preparation had paid off. It was one of the best cricketing days of my life. Winning the two one-day trophies had been great but this was our holy grail and after winning it we got the taste for it. If you can win it once, why not win it again?

The Championship took on a new format for the start of the 2000 season. We had two divisions for the first time and there would be home and away games. Nine teams in each division, so one less game, 16 in all. As defending Champions we knew the value of a fast start. The squad hadn't changed and as Saqi would be available for 12 games this year, the omens looked good – until, that is, we started playing cricket. After three games we hadn't looked like winning a match. We lost to the perennial whipping boys, Durham, at the Riverside and were bottom of the table. So much for defending your title.

The game against Hampshire at The Oval took on major significance. Shane Warne was playing county cricket for the first time and would have a considerable influence on the game. We batted first and got up to 333, a good score. In reply Hampshire limped up to 210, before we in turn started to struggle against Warne and Mullally. To be bowled out for 142 on a flat pitch showed our form to date was pretty patchy. Chasing 265 to win, Hampshire stuttered all the way and despite a 50 from Warne the game was in the bag. At 173-9, they still needed an improbable 92 to win. We were all bowling well and it was only a matter of time before the last wicket fell. But we took it too much for granted and our foot came off the gas. A little last-wicket partnership developed between Mascarenhas and Francis that got them a bit closer – and then some more. We were starting to feel the pressure. We took the new ball – but nothing, not even a chance. They grew in confidence and whittled down the required runs. Tea came along with five runs required to win. It was all over. We had nothing left in the tank. Our season was going to be over before it had started; another loss would have left us a mountain to climb.

After tea they took a couple of singles and with two to win Mascarenhas turned down a single. He wanted to hit the winning runs, to play the big shot and be the hero. He messed up. Trying to pull a ball from Alex Tudor all he succeeded in doing was top edge it up in the air. After what felt like an eternity the ball came down to rest in Alex's hands. He was off, sprinting around the ground like he had scored the winning goal in a cup final. I couldn't get near him, I didn't have the energy. The emotions you go through in sport and situations like that are just something else. But that, in part, is why we play the game.

If that game was supposed to kick start our season, it was a false dawn. A trip to Derby followed. Derbyshire, led by Dominic Cork employed the 'little club versus big club' mentality when they played us. Preparing another damp wicket to negate Saqi and Sals they beat us. Tim Munton, not in the prime of his career by any stretch of the imagination, came in, dropped it on a length and let the pitch take over. He got 7-34 and we were bowled out for just 138. We fought back hard but lost the game by seven wickets. The newly-formed pitch inspectors came in to look at the pitch. They had the power to dock points if they thought the pitch was sub-standard and they did so, rightly in everyone's opinion except Derby's.

All hell broke loose. Derby accused us of influencing the pitch inspectors. The bottom line is we lost the match and were bottom of the table. It wasn't looking too clever. With Cork in control at Derby, more fun and games followed. We had stayed up in Derby for the Sunday League game and wanted to practise on the day off. We arrived at the ground to find our dressing room had been locked and no one could find the key. We were also banned from training on the ground. All this because they prepared a crap pitch! The Sunday League game was also a little bit feisty. The dressing room is right next to the members' bar and there were flash points all day. It was good to leave at the end of the match.

Something had to happen in our season, and it had to happen fast. Our next set of fixtures didn't look the easiest on paper but I kept looking at the league table and I couldn't see anyone who could win the league. If we got a little run going, we could get ourselves in a position to really challenge. A little run followed; we won seven games in a row. It was possibly the best display of ruthless cricket I have ever played in. We were just awesome – no close games, just dominance of the opposition.

We played Leicester twice in that period, once at Oakham School where Ali Brown scored an incredible 295 not out to get us out of a bit of trouble at 190-7. The beauty of our team was that everyone could bat. In Bicknell, Salisbury, Tudor and Saqi you had numbers 8-11 all capable of scoring hundreds. With Browny scoring at one end you had Saqi at the other scoring 66, at number 11. Leicester were put away with ease, an innings victory underlying our superiority over them. The return game at Guildford a couple of weeks later would be different for another reason.

Guildford had become a good ground for us. A run of victories over the previous five years meant we always looked forward to coming back to the ground. For me personally, it was my favourite ground. Living quite close and being a Guildford boy meant that I always had good support. I had played for Guildford for a number of years and it really felt like a home coming every time I stepped onto the field.

We lost the toss on a very good-looking pitch. I managed to get a couple of early wickets and the ball felt like it was coming out really well. It was hard going though – a really hot day – and with no Tudor at the other end the bulk of the overs were bowled by me and Saqi. We gradually made progress through their innings and despite a great innings of 102 from Ben Smith we eventually bowled them out for 318. I took 7-72 from 28 overs; I couldn't have bowled any better. In reply we were going well until checked by Jimmy Ormond's top spell. All out for 288 felt like a kick in the teeth when we had been 266-5. None of the tail scored any runs for a change. Exhausted from the first innings I took the field again. A deficit of 20 was not something we had been used to in recent games and in all honesty I thought we could be in for a real struggle.

The end I normally bowl at had a huge hole where Anil Kumble had been landing his front foot. I have real issues with bad foot holes and contemplated switching ends, except that the other end was just as bad. I decided I would have to get really close into the stumps to avoid the hole. It didn't feel very comfortable until I bowled the perfect delivery to remove Darren Maddy's off stump, pitching on leg stump before swinging away. Another good ball followed to remove Ian Sutcliffe and all of a sudden the game came alive. It was just one of those sessions where it all happens. I bowl it, they edge it and we catch it. With Carl Greenidge getting rid of Ben Smith with the last ball of the day Leicester were 33-6 and I had five wickets. I went home that night thinking something special was going to happen. I had taken 12 of the 16 wickets to fall in the match. Another couple tomorrow would be great, and more importantly we would win the match. The next day was just a carry on from the night before; I managed to grab the last four wickets to finish with 16 in the match, a joint record with Tony Lock, the Surrey spinner from the great 1950s team. We knocked off the 119 with ease; it was all too good to be true. The game ended in just over two days and I got some stick from Guildford cricket club about ruining the festival and their bar takings. It was good to get a day off though. The games were coming thick and fast and we knew we had to keep winning.

Darren's move to Notts was going well for him. He had settled into their team well and they had got themselves a very good player. We have always been very close as brothers and I felt for him having to make that career choice. We knew we would end up playing against each other – but not when or where it was going to happen. By fate, it turned out to be at Guildford in a Sunday League match on a ground where we both grew up, in front of family and friends. Coming so soon after the Leicester match I was still extremely tired and had very little energy to give to the match. The older I got, the harder I found it to 'get up' for one-day games. Any excuse for a day off to save me for the next match was gratefully welcomed, especially at this stage of the season. However, this was one match I wasn't going to miss.

In a situation like this – a one off – the bowler has a slight advantage. One mistake from a batter and it's all over, but bowlers can afford the odd bad ball. Darren was nervous, I could tell that much. I was trying to give it everything I had, but on the day he won. I couldn't get him out. In time I would probably get the better of him but for now part of me just wanted him to do well. He had a lot of family watching him.

Back in the Championship we swept past Lancashire and Derby at The Oval with relative ease. Gary Butcher took four wickets in four balls and Saqi took 7-11 in the second innings against Derby. Clearly they didn't appreciate a dry wicket. That was seven wins out of seven in the Championship and next on the agenda was a trip to Scarborough to play Yorkshire, our closest rivals. The game would go a long way to decide the outcome of the league. I was struggling with a back injury so missed the match. I was gutted. We knew that victory there would effectively win us the league and so did Yorkshire. Underhand tactics would again come to the fore. Call it gamesmanship if you like. I called it cheating.

We turned up on the morning of the game and inspected the pitch. We knew that because of the success of Saqi and Sals – and me not playing – they would leave some grass on the pitch. It would also be a bit damp; they had to take the risk of being deducted points. But the grass on the pitch was literally blowing in the wind it was so long. We lost the toss and obviously we were put into bat. After the lesson we learnt a couple of years previously at Headingley we were now better equipped to deal with pitches away from The Oval. We batted very well to score 356 all out on day one. In testing conditions all the batsmen contributed as we adopted a siege mentality. Arriving at the ground on day two we could see the groundsman cutting the pitch, getting it ready for the day's play. There was grass flying everywhere. We went out and had a look at the pitch to find that all the grass that was on the pitch yesterday had been removed. It was nothing short of disgraceful. Relations between the two sets of players had deteriorated so much that David Byas, the Yorkshire captain, had told his players not to sit anywhere near us at lunch. It was all getting a bit childish. Even with less grass on the pitch Alex Tudor and Ben Hollioake ripped through the Yorkshire line-up to bowl them out for 158. The game was up for Yorkshire. It rained and with the home side struggling to save the game the covers mysteriously disappeared from parts of the square, preventing play from getting back under way. The events at Scarborough were a scandal. They did get docked eight points for an unfit pitch but the ECB really should have thrown them out of Division One for what happened.

With two games to go we knew it was virtually all over. A win at home to Durham would mean another couple of points and would seal it. Ward and Butcher put on 359 for the first wicket and all we had to do was knock them over twice to win the game. Durham were still a very poor side back then and we knew if we had time left in the game we would win easily. Rain played a bit of a part in delaying the inevitable but once the sun came out and Salisbury got to work it was all over bar the shouting. We got the bonus point we needed at Old Trafford against Lancashire but the celebrations had long since started.

We had done it again, but this time we did it the hard way. To have such a bad start and come back playing great cricket made it all the more satisfying. Our one-day form still left a bit to be desired but once again, the Championship was ours.

A lot of our success was down to the fact we had two quality spinners in our side. Playing at The Oval you need to have plenty of variety in your attack and in Saqi and Sals we had that in abundance. Saqi as I have mentioned before was just amazing. Batsmen were clueless how to deal with him. Sals provided the variety at the other end, with an ability to get the very best players out. Sals took his fair share of criticism from Surrey supporters over the years, but his role in Surrey's success cannot be overestimated. Without doubt he bowled the best googly in the world, so few batsmen picked it. Whenever you saw a batsman shaping up to cut the ball you knew it was a googly, and invariably it hit the pads and induced an appeal. However, I always felt with Sals that he needed to have a quality spinner the other end. Whether it was his lack of confidence in himself I don't know, but when he was the sole spinner in the side he generally struggled. I can understand how difficult bowling leg spin is. Not many people have mastered it. But it always struck me that he would have too many reasons for things not going so well. There was no need for it really. When he bowled well he was brilliant, but he just didn't back himself enough.

# No Call-Up, More Trophies and Tragedy Again

On the back of two Championships in a row Surrey County Cricket Club weren't going to stand still. Ed Giddins was signed from Warwickshire, but the biggest signing was that of Mark Ramprakash. Ramps had grown disillusioned at Middlesex. A spell being captain hadn't worked out and he wanted a move to a club with ambition. I had grown up playing against Ramps but didn't really ever get to know him that well. Even when we played against each other at county level we didn't really gel. Early on in his career everyone knew you could wind him up a bit, get under his skin and induce a false shot. In recent times though we had felt the wrath of his bat. A couple of double hundreds confirmed that he was a dominant player in county cricket.

I felt it was a great signing – more so than signing Giddens. Giddens had more baggage than Heathrow. A spell out of the game as a result of a drugs ban merely confirmed he was a bit of a gamble. He was a fine bowler though, and we were under strength in that department. With Alex Tudor still injury prone and Ben Hollioake not having fulfilled his talent, we needed a bit more quality. But Giddens never really 'did it' at Surrey – a spell in the Benson and Hedges final aside. I think Surrey got him a couple of years too late.

We were definitely the team to beat and we started the season as massive favourites to make it three in a row. The early games, once again wrecked by bad weather didn't really worry us. As time went on we just couldn't get going. We didn't play poorly as 11 draws out of 16 games will tell you, but we couldn't convert enough of those games into wins. It wasn't until the sixth game that we won one in the Championship, and another four before we rolled over Northants at Guildford. With the Championship being two divisions, of which three teams from nine get relegated we were looking over our shoulder.

My own form just got better and better. My stats for the 2001 season were probably the best of my career. Seventy-two wickets at 21 per wicket, and 748 runs at an average of 46 per innings, elevating me to all rounder status. I scored my maiden first-class hundred at Canterbury and revelled in my position in the team. With so many players struggling for form I felt extra responsibility for keeping us in the First Division. 2001 will probably go down as the year of one of my biggest achievements – keeping Surrey in the top flight. There were other awards though. I was named one of Wisden Criceters of the Year, and Surrey's Players' Player of the Year for the fifth year in a row. In the PCA Awards I had come second to David Fulton in 2000 and felt sure that 2001 had to be my year. Again I would miss out, second this time to Marcus Trescothick.

There were certain players I seemed to have a mesmeric hold on. Darren Maddy and Steve James were two guys that I got out for fun. In his book 'Third Man to Fatty's leg' James goes into real detail about the mental battle he had facing me. At the time I didn't give it too much thought, but of all the bowlers in the country he hated facing me above most others. I wasn't quick enough to give him sleepless nights as some bowlers were, but I got the ball into areas that he just wasn't comfortable playing. He also described me as being grumpy and surly on the field. Other people thought I was surly and arrogant as well. To be honest I was always a bit taken aback by these claims. On the field for sure I wasn't going to be too friendly and the thought of having a laugh and a joke with the batsmen would go against the grain. But off it, while I may hold back a little, arrogant I am not. I have never been confident enough to be that.

There was still no sign of an England call. Physically I couldn't do any more to get in the side. Darren Gough and Andrew Caddick were the obstacles in my way and apparently the selectors didn't see me as a first-change bowler. What a load of bollocks. I could have played as an all rounder my stats were that good. What really annoyed me more than anything was the way I was treated though. I didn't have any contact with the selectors – not one phone call explaining the situation. Maybe they felt they didn't need to talk to me, but I still felt hard done by.

I think the incident that summed it all up came at the Benson and Hedges final at Lord's against Gloucestershire. England were in the middle of the series against Australia, and of course it wasn't going so well. Lord's traditionally favours swing bowlers and the rumour mill was once again in overdrive with talk about me. This time though it was a bit different. Alec Stewart, who knew a few things when it came to England selections, told me I was virtually assured of a place. We were in the middle of preparation for the final so it was a distraction I didn't really need. However, I was quite excited by the talk and the attention.

The final was played out on the Saturday. We won, and the newspaper guys seemed to know I was going to be named in the squad. When we were changing in the home dressing room Alec even told me to leave my kit there for the following week. Winning the final was one thing, but to play for England the following week would be pretty special.

After the final we stayed in London for the celebrations. I woke fairly gingerly on the Sunday morning and put my phone on, waiting for it to ring. It was still quite early so I wasn't overly worried at this point; we had breakfast but still nothing. I knew the team was to be announced at 11am so we left the hotel and went to the ground to kill some time. 11am came and went. Something wasn't right. An announcement came over the radio saying there was a delay in naming the squad. I had a sinking feeling. Deep down I knew I wasn't in. No phone call, no nothing. The announcement came out at 12am. On the back of his three wickets in the final, Alex Tudor, was in. There was no M Bicknell in the list. Gutted doesn't even begin to describe my feelings. I had bowled beautifully for five years. I had scored plenty of runs. I had lost the 'always injured' tag and helped Surrey to win after win, trophy after trophy. The selectors had changed their minds on the back of a one-day game. It just summed up my feelings towards the England selectors; they could go to hell as far as I was concerned. I was happy playing for Surrey and couldn't give a toss about playing for England any more. That was it.

I had a chat with Keith Medlycott during the Yorkshire game at Headingley. I wanted to put out a statement saying I was not available for

England selection anymore. It didn't really matter because they obviously weren't going to pick me anyway, but it would make me feel better. Without that distraction I could get on with Surrey business and put all the England stuff away once and for all. He advised me against it and said it was just a reaction to being overlooked again and there was no need to be so hasty. He was right. I was just being angry; I wanted to make a statement of how hurt I was. I wasn't the only cricketer to be overlooked by England, but it sure felt like it at the time.

I guess what really galls me is the fact that not once did I have any contact with David Graveney. He must have known how upset I was – and not just about that one incident but over a long period of time. It is just common courtesy to pick up the phone and let someone know where they stand.

After a while I looked at it two ways. If I wasn't being picked by England I was helping Surrey win trophies. Your club side is your bread and butter, and where my heart is. If England came along, all well and good. I knew I wasn't going to play a hundred Test matches – I knew my level – but if the opportunity came along I knew I was good enough. At least I had played before. Many players, including my brother didn't get one chance. I gave up wishing for another chance – and then of course it arrives, when you least expect it.

We avoided relegation in the Championship by beating Yorkshire in the penultimate game of the season. Yorkshire had just won the title and were in London on a mission to celebrate. They rested several big name players and missed the chance to beat us, and send us down. They would live to regret that moment.

# BICKERS

Our only success in 2001 came in the Benson and Hedges Trophy. We scraped through the group stages and into a quarter-final tie at Hove against Sussex. Browny's perfectly paced hundred gave us enough runs to play with and we came through well. The semi-final would be against Notts, with another encounter with Darren on the agenda. With Jason Gallian injured, Darren had assumed the captaincy for the second half of the year. He ran into a juggernaut and was powerless to do anything about it. I felt sorry for him trying to stem the flow of runs. It was a performance that oozed class and confidence and Notts were crushed by nearly 200 runs. Our side was made up entirely of international cricketers, players who knew how to play in the big matches. We were often accused of being arrogant, strutting around as if we owned the place. In truth, that's exactly how we wanted to be perceived. We did own the pitch; we wanted to give off the aura of invincibility. We were Surrey, like us or loathe us.

The final brought together the two best one-day sides in the country. Gloucestershire had won just about everything in one-day terms. In Ian Harvey they had a match winner, and the rest of the team knew their roles to perfection. Jack Russell would stand up to the stumps to all their bowlers, and the fielders would throw the ball in to Jack at every possible opportunity. It was meant to be intimidating, to build up pressure and induce mistakes. The final was seen as the 'all stars' of Surrey against the one-day kings.

We had something up our sleeves though. I suggested in the team meeting before the match that they would throw the ball into Jack and try and get under our skin – even at us if necessary, to wind us up a bit. Ian Ward thought it would be a good idea to get in the way of the throws and deflect the ball away. Early in the game it happened. He hit the ball to mid on and with perfect timing the ball came in to Jack. Wardy stood there, watched the ball, and at the last minute deflected it off his helmet, away from Jack. Immediately there was a reaction from the fielders. They now didn't know what to do so they stopped throwing the ball in. Wardy had got under their skin and they wouldn't be able to intimidate us. We cobbled together a decent score. 244 in 50 overs was good, but was it enough?

We were at them from the start. Alex Tudor bowled three maidens in a row and I supported well the other end. Ed Giddens followed Tudes and bowled the best spell of his Surrey career. We didn't let up and won by 47 runs. It was a near perfect game. Ben Hollioake had played brilliantly again, 73 off 76 balls when our innings was in the balance. Ben was becoming an outstanding cricketer and this innings proved once again that he could cut it at the highest level. It would be his last performance at Lord's.

Ben was a special talent. One of the most gifted cricketers I came across, with talent to burn. It would only be a matter of time before he fulfilled that potential. It wasn't just cricket either. If you went out with Ben into a crowded bar you could look around the room and all the girls would be looking in his direction. He was cool, good-looking and just a lovely bloke. He was laid back and easy going, a real contrast to his brother. They had different qualities but Adam and Ben were really close, although at times you wouldn't know it. They argued like brothers, but underneath they loved each other.

That Friday in March was just another day. I had been training, preparing for a new season. England were playing in Wellington and I had watched the highlights. We had a quiet night in. Just before we were going to bed Loraine took a call from Ian Salisbury's wife, Emma. There had been a car accident in Perth. Ben was dead. Janaya, his girlfriend, in the car at the time, wasn't expected to pull through.

Life doesn't prepare you for things like that, the shock, the anger and the feelings of helplessness. I remember watching England in New Zealand that night. I knew what had happened, but the team hadn't been told the news as yet and I waited and watched as news filtered through to the dressing room. It was awful, the empty look on so many faces. I knew plenty of players who had played with Ben only a few short weeks before. After the Graham Kersey accident in 1997 I hoped I would never have to go through something like that again. And here it was again. How would we deal with this?

We, as players and team-mates gathered at Ian Salisbury's house. Sals and Ben were virtually inseparable. It didn't take long to decide we had to go out to Perth as soon as possible. We had to be there for Adam and his family. We were a very tight unit and the only way to get through this was to be together.

Most of the team went to Perth. It was nearly pre-season but training wasn't on our minds. We arrived and went to the family house. I will never forget the look on John Hollioake's face as long as I shall live. How do you deal with the loss of one of your children? Adam was trying to be strong for everyone but in his eyes, the lights had gone out. We all cried and cried and cried. For five days we cried, at the service and the funeral and more besides. The funeral was one of the saddest days of my life. Adam spoke beautifully, about Ben and there being another life for him. About a day in their family lives when there was Ben, and then there was no Ben. Adam told a story about Ben at school. A bird had flown into the sports hall and was stuck. Ben, seeing the bird in distress, went and got a stone from outside. He threw the stone at the window so the bird could escape. He wasn't interested in the fact that he could get into serious trouble for breaking this massive window, only that the bird wouldn't suffer. That really said it all about Ben. Words cannot describe the emotion in that room. Janaya was still in a coma but her family were there for Ben. Janaya would pull through, but her life without Ben?

Adam wasn't coming back for the start of the 2002 season; he said he might not come back at all. His life was about making sure his family was alright. He had to try and hold it all together while all around him people couldn't cope. Cricket didn't matter in Adam's life anymore.

Back in England there were noises about dedicating the season to Ben, winning something in his name, etc. It just didn't sit right. How can anything help an already desperate situation? We knew we had to get back on the field. Adam and his family wanted that. It is what Ben would have wanted too. It didn't change anything. We had lost Ben and we had also lost our leader, the man responsible for gelling us all together.

First up that season were Sussex. They too found themselves in mourning. Umer Rashid had died in a swimming accident on their pre-season tour. It was a pretty sombre start to the season, a game played at half mast, by players with other things on their minds. We won comfortably and then won the next two games as well. We played pretty awesome cricket, inspired by a variety of things – by last year's disappointment in the Championship, by Yorkshire taking the title off us, and by Ben's loss. This year took on new meaning for all of us. There were far more important things in life than a game of cricket. It put everything into perspective. Worrying about trivialities took a back seat. We all had another outlook on life.

As well as we played in the Championship, our defence of the Benson and Hedges couldn't have started any worse. In Adam's absence cracks began to appear. There was criticism of Keith Medlycott, criticism of the way we approached one-day cricket and general backbiting. It wouldn't have happened had Adam been there. No one questioned his approach to the game, we all sang from the same hymn sheet. The Championship was taking care of itself. A monkey could have captained that side it was so good. But one-day cricket is where you need good leadership and good plans. Medlycott wasn't the same without Adam around. He should have taken the bull by the horns and got hold of the side. But it wasn't his style. He needed a strong leader at the top so he could operate behind him. We needed Adam back.

Adam returned at the start of July. His family had told him to go back and play. He wasn't so sure. We wanted him back, we wanted to help him get through it, he was our mate. But things were different now. Adam played as if nothing mattered, played with a freedom that culminated in 117 not out off 59 balls in the Cheltenham and Gloucester quarter-final against Sussex. It was an awesome display of hitting.

The Championship was taking care of itself. After being in great form for the first six games of the season an injury meant I had the next seven weeks off. Slipping in my follow through in a one-day game at home to Sussex, I broke my right wrist. Excruciating pain told me there was a problem and a spell on the sidelines left me bored and frustrated. It was probably the point where I was never quite the same bowler again. After seven weeks out I came back at Leicester. I was still highly regarded around the country and coming back at a time where we needed to kick on and win the title, my return was seen as a massive boost for the team. But it didn't feel right. I bowled pretty poorly for the rest of the season. Something was missing, I had lost a yard of pace, felt very unfit, and for the first time in ages I wasn't able to influence the game as I used to. I was getting older and I started to doubt myself again. I hated it.

We won the Championship at a canter. Ian Ward scored 1,700 runs with seven hundreds, Ramps scored another three hundreds and Jimmy Ormond and Saqi both took 50 wickets. Three Championships in four years emphasised our dominance in the country. If we played well we would win. However, the cracks were getting wider. We were an ageing side, opinionated and with quite a few expanding egos. We had too many top players. It sounds a bit odd but the team balance didn't feel right. Guys like Nadeem Shahid couldn't get a game. Someone like him should have played more games for Surrey. The best short leg in the country, Saqi and Sals were always grateful to have him in there. It's nice to have 11 internationals in your side but it doesn't necessarily make it a team.

Being successful brings its own problems. Players want more money, want to play every game, to lead the side, and have their own opinions on who should be playing. The returning Test players, as good as they were, became a burden to the side. Jon Batty would step down for Alec Stewart, Ricki Clarke would miss out after scoring a hundred and there would be countless other occasions where a player would feel hard done by. It didn't help team spirit.

# BICKERS

2003 arrived with more expectation. The team had stayed together, a year older and fading, but still good enough to dominate. Off the field, cracks were widening further. Adam was having private issues with Janaya and her parents about money. Incredibly this issue became the subject of rumour and gossip in the dressing room. It should have been no one's business but theirs, but too many people had an opinion and it created divisions. My loyalties were firmly with Adam. That isn't to say I didn't understand the complexities of the situation, but Adam and I were, and still are, quite close.

It was the beginning of the end. Adam got sick of it, the off-field stuff, the backbiting and the relentless grind of being captain. By the end of 2003 I think he wanted to call it a day. He stepped down from being captain but would have one more year just as a player.

We didn't lose a single game until the quarter-final C&G defeat at Derby on 11th June. We were leading the Championship, smashing everybody in sight in the National League Division One, and would go on to win the newly-formed Twenty20. Yet it was an unhappy dressing room. Bitching and backbiting ruled the roost. Someone wasn't happy with someone else, the coach wasn't doing his job properly, and the youngsters were lazy. Even Adam took criticism for the laid-back approach he and Medlycott had adopted. But we kept winning, we had good players, good players who knew how to win.

I found the going a little tough at the start of the season. My run-up wasn't right, the ball wasn't coming out well enough and perhaps time was catching up with me. I decided to experiment a bit. In the game against Notts at Trent Bridge I went wicketless in the first innings. I bowled

# Martin Bicknell

OK but got tired in my second spell. I used to have a very long run-up. I had tried to change it in the past but it just hadn't worked. Now things were a bit different. I was older and not able to do the things I used to do. At the start of the second innings I marked out a shorter run-up, ran through it a few times and it felt quite comfortable. Darren was opening the batting for Notts. The first ball came out OK, with a bit more pace than the first innings. "This feels good", I think to myself. Another couple of balls and the ball is flying through to Alec behind the stumps. The fifth ball comes out beautifully, with a little inswing and nails him plumb in front of all three. D Bicknell LBW Bowled M Bicknell 0, I can't tell you what that meant. I didn't want to gloat about getting him out so I ran past him without looking in his direction. For the rest of the innings I feel like a new bowler, more pace, good control and five wickets. I left Trent Bridge in the knowledge that I had found something to get me back to my best, something that would eventually get me back into the Test side.

The Twenty20 started in 2003. I think as players we were all a bit sceptical about it until we played in front of 10,000 people at The Oval against Middlesex. It suited us perfectly, a team of big hitters and clever one-day bowlers. I didn't play an awful lot, rested a bit, but when I did play enjoyed it and bowled well. Finals day at Nottingham and I am fully expecting to play. We watch the first semi-final and the ball turns for the spinners. I still have no idea that I am not going to play until Adam puts his arm around me and explains they will be playing Saqi and Sals. I feel gutted to miss out on such a big occasion but I understand the situation. The team plays superbly and an inspired spell from Jimmy Ormond destroys Warwickshire in the final and the Cup is ours. In the celebrations

# BICKERS

I have a slightly hollow feeling. I have played a major part in all the trophies we have won so far, but now I am on the periphery, looking in. It's a strange feeling.

The Surrey wheels finally fell off at Leicester. I had been selected for England, so was unavailable. I wanted to help Surrey win the title though and Leicester would be crucial. After dominating the game we ran into a brick wall as Leicester scored 636-4 in their second innings – this after following on having made just 166 in the first innings. The failure to win that game knocked the stuffing out of the team. We were competing on all fronts, playing big games week after week and the fight went out of us. A defeat at Lancashire in the next championship match summed up the situation perfectly. After fighting back into the game to draw level on first innings, we folded in the second. There was nothing left in the tank, and not much leadership at the top. The laid-back approach was now biting us on the arse; it was open debate on whether we were doing enough hard work? Were we preparing properly? Had we taken our eye off the ball?

When you lose, people look for reasons and excuses. Was it the coach's fault, was it the captain's? Who can I blame? More often than not, if you look in the mirror you get your answer. The team had stopped working hard. The younger players came into a very successful side and saw senior players take their foot off the gas and cruise around, expecting to win, and this rubbed off on them. Dedicated practisers, like Ian Ward and Mark Ramprakash, took issue with some of the younger guys for not doing enough, and rightly so. But this created more problems and added to the internal bickering, as so often happens when a team is in trouble. I think as a team we were all to blame. We had a lazy attitude to practice and preparation and this had to be addressed. Adam and Keith Medlycott had adopted a relaxed attitude to things. The players were expected to look after themselves and take responsibility for preparation. We were, after all, senior, experienced cricketers. When things are going well, as they had been for much of the previous five seasons, people go with the flow. But when things start going off the rails, inquests begin and blame is attached. Reasons for failure are found and the first thing people look at is preparation – and ours was average to say the least.

It is easy to forget that we won two trophies that year. We did blow the Championship, eventually finishing third as Sussex won their first title. It was the end for us as a Championship force. Saqi had lost a bit of his sparkle. I would never really recapture my best form and others were on the wrong side of 30. We did well in the one-day arena, but at the end of the season I walked away from the ground feeling a little empty. Things had changed. It felt like the end of an era. The side we had built up was breaking up. Our captain and inspiration had effectively gone and things were about to change… for the worse.

# England Call Again

So, just when you think it couldn't possibly happen again it does. I'm having a quiet nap on the sofa during a day off and awake to hear my messages on my mobile. It's David Graveney – asking me to give him a call on his mobile. England had just beaten South Africa at Trent Bridge on a terrible wicket with James Kirtley taking a bag full of wickets. What on earth would David Graveney want to call me for? I didn't call him straight back. In a way I wanted to work out why he was calling me. I thought it might be to discuss a seam bowler who could be in the frame. Graveney wasn't in the habit of calling me for a chat; to be honest I wasn't sure he even had my number after the times I had thought he might call me. I left it a good hour before I started to dial his number and by this stage I was thinking the unthinkable. Could it be? Ten years after my last appearance was I going to have another crack at it? Just as I was about to press the call button I had a call from Shilpa Patel. Shilpa heads up the Test Match Special production and when she asked me for an interview the game was up. I phoned Grav. He said I would be required to travel up to Leeds where I might be needed depending on the fitness of Steve Harmison.

My immediate thought was "you bastard, why wait until I'm 34, past my best and without a great future at Test level to pick me?" If I play and it all goes wrong people can turn around and say "I told you he wasn't good enough to play at this level" and if it goes well Graveney gets a pat on the back for an excellent selection. On the one hand I was so excited I was shaking and on the other I was seriously bewildered. Why now? What if I make a fool out of myself? Do I really need this? For the last 10 years I have made one hell of a reputation for myself in the county game. Does it really need to be tarnished with a fleeting visit back on the international stage when I am past my best? Sure, five years ago when I was at the peak of my game you could have given me a crack. But now, do me a favour! Are South Africa going to be worried about a 34-year-old medium pacer who is slightly injury prone and liable to break down at any moment?

Word gets round pretty quickly. My phone went mad. People I hadn't heard from for ages were calling me, just on the off chance of a complimentary ticket. Cheeky bastards! I was on my way in to The Oval anyway to pick up some kit and it was there I was to do all the customary interviews with TV and radio. Things had certainly moved on in the 10 years I had been away. The press and TV interest were amazing. It felt pretty good to be this popular, even though it was at the back of my mind I really didn't think it was a good idea in the first place. What were the selectors thinking of? I did the usual round of interviews and went home to pack.

I travelled to Leeds the next day. By now I had read all the papers and there was a pretty common theme developing. It was very much a horses for courses selection, and in all likelihood, a one off. Steve Harmison had been suffering with a sore back and it was made out that I was there as his 'cover'. I had a nagging thought in the back of my mind though that I might play anyway, with or without him.

# BICKERS

My form for Surrey had been OK; we had just finished a game at Whitgift School in Croydon against Nottinghamshire where I had taken eight wickets in the match. The ball had come out of my hand beautifully all game. The pitch had pace and bounce, but crucially the ball had swung – all the ingredients I needed to take wickets. At this stage of my career I needed a few things in my favour to perform at my best. Low, slow pitches where the ball barely carries to the keeper really did not suit my bowling, especially with the loss of a yard of pace. I had even cut my run-up down at the start of the season. I used to run in at least 30 yards, but the onset of old age had meant if I was to be able to bowl three spells a day I was going to have to conserve a bit of energy. In short, being 34 I should have been thinking about retiring, not playing for England.

Arriving in Leeds I felt like a fish out of water. I was so used to doing the county thing and knowing everyone, this was all alien to me. The press attention, the hype around the Test team, and getting kitted out in all the England stuff again. I had been in my comfort zone for so long in county cricket; you can understand why some people never fully get to grips with the transition from county cricket to Test cricket. All the attention and intrusion into your life can just be too much for some people. When you play for England your technique is taken apart by all and sundry. Any flaw you have will be ruthlessly exposed and if you haven't got a thick enough skin these things can have a dangerously detrimental effect on your career. I really believe you need to get off to a great start in international cricket to succeed. You need look no further than Strauss, Cook and Prior to see what a great advantage it is to start well and have that belief that you can cut it at the top level. Guys like Mark Ramprakash and Graeme Hick started poorly and didn't go on to be the top England players they should have been.

I was fortunate to know most of the players in the England side and they made me feel very welcome. Nasser Hussain had stood down recently and Michael Vaughan had taken over and won his first Test in charge. Nasser was known to most as a fairly prickly character. I had known Nass since we played in the England Under 19 team together and we got on well. It was widely acknowledged though that he had a side to him that wasn't the most pleasant and he had a habit of getting on the wrong side of people. His captaincy and body language on the field also drew some comment. Nass was hugely passionate about his country and couldn't understand why people didn't show the same desire to win as he did. That I can understand, but understanding that no one is the same as you are is part of being a great captain and an area that Nass really didn't come to terms with. I sure as hell wouldn't have liked him standing at mid off when I was bowling and giving me a hard time for bowling a bad ball, as he so often did to the England bowlers. That you can do without.

Michael Vaughan on the other hand was a totally different character. A very calm man with a great tactical brain. In the games I played for England he had an easygoing manner about him that had a great settling effect, especially on me. He was more my type of captain. I was fortunate enough to play under Adam Hollioake for a long time, for me the best captain I played under, and it was great to see Vaughan go on to become one of the world's best.

One man I did feel wary about was Duncan Fletcher. In all the years I had been in the frame to play for England I had a pretty good idea who was in the 'no' camp on my selection. I knew I wasn't his choice to be in the squad so it would be interesting to see how he would treat me. I didn't know him at all and he is a man who says little. I wasn't going to lose any sleep over it; there was quite enough other stuff going on anyway.

The biggest thing I was worried about before playing was the bloody 'speed gun'. Not the thing on the roads, but the device with which they measure your bowling speed. Now, I have never been blessed with express pace, and at 34 had certainly lost another yard, but this really concerned me. Over the years this one thing had been thrown at me time and time again as the reason I had not been selected. "You can't get good players out without bowling 90mph" seemed to be the mantra of the 1990s. 'Bollocks' has generally been my response. And when I see Shaun Pollock, Chaminda Vaas and Glenn McGrath operating around the 80mph mark with great success, you can see where my frustration comes from. (I for one was definitely an advocate of picking Ryan Sidebottom last year – an excellent swing bowler with a very good county record who had a great 2007 taking wickets on the international stage with what I would call old-fashioned bowling. Pitch it up and let it swing. Congratulations must of course go to Peter Moores; a man who clearly doesn't live by the theory if you can't knock someone's head off you won't be successful at national level. If you are a good bowler you are a good bowler, end of conversation. But the speed gun really concerned me. In the county game whenever the TV cameras turn up, so does the speed gun. All the bowlers are conscious of it; they want to be the fastest bowler on show. They all try that little bit harder and have a look at the timings. I just wanted respectability – somewhere in the high 70s would be OK.

# Martin Bicknell

Practice had gone well over the couple of days. I had been very impressed with Troy Cooley, the then England bowling coach. So much is made of new coaching techniques and theories but essentially the game does not change. I am a firm believer in keeping the game as simple as possible and so is Cooley. I can see why the England bowlers had such a good relationship with him. Too much information clutters your head. We are cricketers not rocket scientists.

As the start of the game drew nearer I was starting to get the feeling I was going to be in the team. Surrey were due to play at Leicester in a crucial Championship match and I was sorry to miss it. If I was left out I could get down there later in the day. The Surrey boys had been flying all season and were on course for a treble, despite all the internal trouble brewing. I had other things on my mind though, like not tripping up running in to bowl on national TV.

It's the night before the Test starts and we have gone through the usual team meeting and discussions about opposition players. Shaun Pollock has gone back home for the birth of his first child so he will be missed. The pitch looks average to say the least. We will probably play four seamers. As it turned out we would play five – a bizarre decision. Harmison doesn't look right despite what he says about being OK to play. Harmison at this stage still hadn't really cut it at Test level. A hugely talented bowler, he dislikes being away from home. His time would come soon enough though.

It's the morning of the game and nerves are getting the better of me. I get the nod. I am playing. Giles and Harmison miss out, South Africa win the toss and bat. Half an hour to go before the start of the game and the feeling is incredible. Here I am, back on the biggest stage and it's make or break time. Bowl like an idiot and let down all the people championing my cause over the last 10 years, or make a name for myself and stick two fingers up at all the people who doubted me for so long. We get off to the perfect start. James Kirtley, running down the hill, gets Graeme Smith to nick one to Alec Stewart. My initial thought is I am glad I don't have to bowl to him after the way he has savaged England's attack for most of the summer. My turn now; running up the hill with a strong wind at my back, bowling to Herschelle Gibbs. The first ball comes out well, but not as well as the second. It's as if it's all in slow motion as Gibbs nicks the ball through to Alec Stewart and pandemonium breaks out. Bloody hell, I have another Test wicket and South Africa are 2-2! I struggle to hold it all together. To think I wasn't sure if I deserved to be here. It gets better; the pitch is doing plenty and Kallis is next to go. After my first spell I have 2-9. I have to keep pinching myself; there cannot be any greater feeling in cricket than doing well for your country. Even if it all goes pear-shaped from here, at least I have made a mark. At lunch I daren't even turn my mobile on; I know there are going to be stacks of messages. Ashley Giles left a little note for me saying congrats before he left to go back and play for his county side. Ashley and I go back a long way. I dated his sister when I was 16. Giles was 12 then and just loved his cricket. Bowling medium pace, he never really looked like making the grade until one day, playing for Guildford, he gave left-arm spin a go. The rest is history as they say. It was a very nice gesture to leave the note, and typical of the guy.

The rest of the day is pretty much a blur. At 142-7 we are in the box seat, but a brilliant innings by Gary Kirsten and an unorthodox one by Monde Zondeki rescue the South Africans and eventually they reach 342 all out. My suspect hamstring is causing me a little concern and I don't bowl after tea on the first day. At the end of the innings though I have got through 27 overs and taken 2-50. The ball has moved around a lot and I could have had five wickets. It's so draining though, all the attention, the interviews and the pressure of the situation. I sleep well. We bat well for a time and reach 169-1 before losing Trescothick and Butcher in quick succession. Eventually we get bowled out for 307, not good in view of where we were at one point.

At the start of the second innings we have gathered on the outfield in our huddle as you normally do, and Graeme Smith is walking to the wicket. Andrew Flintoff suddenly breaks away from our group and launches a tirade of abuse in Smith's direction. Smith gives as good as he gets and clearly there is no love lost in that department. Tensions are running high and when I swing one back into Smith's pads to trap him LBW for 14, Headingly erupts. Smith is sent on his way by Flintoff and I have got the main man. I needed to prove the first innings wasn't just a one off and I have done it. The rest of the third day's play is Test cricket at its best. Every ball is an event. It feels a world away from the relatively cosy world of county cricket and I love it. This is what I should have been doing all my career, not in the twilight of it. At one point I catch a glimpse of the big TV screen in the corner of the ground. They are showing a replay of the previous six balls I have bowled to Zondeki. All six balls do something different and he doesn't hit any of them. The commentators are clearly talking about the movement I am getting, I must be impressing them. The pitch is really helping my bowling and in truth I should have taken more than the two I finish up with in the second innings. The South Africans now have a huge lead due to Andrew Hall taking advantage of our tiring attack, and we are left chasing 400 on a wearing pitch. It proves too much and we lose. That's played three Tests lost three Tests for me – and England are down 2-1 in the series.

I had done well though; the pitch had really suited my bowling and if it was all to be a one off at least I could walk away knowing I had not let anyone down. I had enhanced my reputation in the game and if that was it I could go back to Surrey and finish my career knowing I'd had a great experience. There was however another surprise when I was named in the next squad for the game to be played at The Oval. It was to be the last Test of the series, and on my home ground. Now, The Oval isn't like Headingley. It is widely accepted as one of the best batting pitches in the country. As a bowler your margin for error is so small that if you don't bowl well you can disappear all over the ground. After Leeds, this would be a much, much bigger test.

In the week after the Headingley Test match I had to have intensive treatment on my hamstring injury. It wasn't anything massive, but it was causing me problems when I had to run in hard to the crease. At the back of my mind was the thought that if I wasn't 100% fit to play there was no way I could risk it. Break down in the middle of a Test match and let England down? No way. In my negative way of thinking I also worried that I would struggle to take wickets on a great batting pitch like The Oval. It wouldn't be such a bad thing to sit this one out and not risk being destroyed by the media for a poor performance. I had had my go on a pitch that suited me and I'd done well. I wasn't going to go on tour to Bangladesh anyway.

# Martin Bicknell

Then the other, slightly more positive side of my brain kicked in. This is The Oval, your home ground; you have earned another crack at the big time. Stop being so ridiculous and get fit. You won't get another chance. All my family and friends would be there. They have waited a long time for this as well, a chance for them to share the moment.

I proved my game fitness back at Leeds against Yorkshire. Vaughan batted very well but we won again to take the National League One-Day title. It was the second of two trophies we would win that year. We should have won three, the Championship eluding us as we crashed and burned at the back end of the season. For so long we had dominated the county game and to win three trophies in a year would have been something special, but it wasn't to be. My being called up by England didn't help the Surrey cause but the trouble that was brewing in the team was probably the major factor. As a team, with a couple of exceptions, we had become lazy. This didn't help the young guys coming into the side who were given the impression that county cricket was quite easy. We took our foot off the gas and got caught out.

Test match practice is for you to report back three days before the start of the game. With there still being a bit of a doubt over my hamstring I was there early, doing a bit of training while the ground was quiet. The adrenaline was building, even with no one at the ground. Graham Thorpe was back in the team for Hussain, who had broken a toe at Leeds. Thorpey and I have had what I would call a strange relationship. We first played cricket together at the age of 10 and came up through the ranks. We played football for the same team as well so you would think we would be quite close, but no. I think we are quite similar characters in a way, quite introverted, have our own group of friends and don't mix that well with people we don't know. But Thorpey is very much his own man and has a selfish streak that has probably served him well over the years. I don't know of many people it has endeared him to though.

We are staying at the Grange Hotel by Tower Bridge. It is where David Blaine is trying to live in a plastic cage, so attention around the area is vast, and bemusing. It would also be the scene of something more bizarre later in the week. Alec Stewart is having a Testimonial dinner two days before the match and all the England players go. We are treated like royalty; this is the life. I see lots of people I know, all wishing me well and saying well done. I know I have to play in this game now. Seeing what it means to other people is enough for me. David Graveney collars me at one point and basically tells me if I am not 100% fit don't even think about playing. His job is on the line. No pressure there then.

South Africa win the toss again and have no hesitation in batting. James Kirtley is injured, so Steve Harmison comes in, as does Ashley Giles for Kabir Ali. I get to bowl the first over of the game to Graeme Smith. It's a maiden but I know it's going to be a long day and so it proves. The pitch is flat and the ball doesn't swing and I look, and feel, innocuous. Towards the end of the first day I can hear the England crowd getting restless and having a go at some of our players. I just want the game to be over; it feels like a bridge too far for me. I haven't bowled well and we are getting murdered. All I can think of is what the press will make of it. We live in an age of intense criticism and the next day's papers are fairly savage. Two late wickets help, but South Africa are 362-4 and on for a huge score.

As I came to the ground the following morning I decided to stop worrying about what people were thinking and just go out and enjoy the occasion. I deliberately didn't read the papers which I knew would be quite scathing. I didn't want that negativity in my head before the start of the day's play. Michael Vaughan sprang a surprise on me and gave me the ball at the start of the day to see if it might swing. I repaid his faith immediately to have Jacques Rudolph LBW with a good inswinger. With the ball swinging I was right in the game now. Boucher nicked one to Alec and it was game on. I was a different bowler from the day before. Isn't it amazing how a bit of success can change your outlook on life. The crowd really got behind us and we turned the game around. A late flurry from Pollock meant South Africa reached 484, a big total. However, the way that Trescothick got after their bowling meant that total might be within reach. Thorpey in his comeback match also got in on the act with a hundred and Flintoff, now revelling in his new-found notoriety, butchered the tiring attack with a stunning 95. A lead of 120 would be just enough to put some doubt into their minds in a game they really should have killed off long ago.

Once again with the new ball in hand I ran in hard and gave it everything, Trescothick dropped Gibbs off me but Anderson got him the other end. With a sold out crowd roaring me on, I trapped Smith in front. The crowd erupted. That Sunday at The Oval was without doubt the best day's cricket of my life. I couldn't have bowled any better. We were all over the South Africans and I got Rudolph out with the oldest trick in the book. Two outswingers which he left, and then an inswinger to knock back his off stump. For that trick to work on the biggest stage of all, in front of my home crowd – it's hard to describe the feelings. The day couldn't have gone any better. They were only 65 ahead with only four wickets left. We knew there was hard work still to be done, but tomorrow we could level the series.

The expectation coming to the ground on the Monday morning was something else; I knew this would be my last day's Test cricket, as it would be also for Alec Stewart who would be retiring after 131 Test matches. The day started well and I removed Boucher and Hall in successive deliveries. Bloody hell I'm thinking, I could take five here. But Harmison mopped up the other two to leave us chasing just over a hundred. It was easy. Trescothick guided us home and the champagne flowed. I was so tired. It had been emotionally draining and physically tough too. I had got through nearly 50 overs on a flat wicket, but that was to be nothing compared to the test of stamina that drinking with Flintoff and Butcher would be as we celebrated!

Nothing compares with doing well for your country – to the sense of achievement in helping your country win a Test match, especially at your home ground. I had finally played in a winning Test side; after three losses finally a win – and what a win. Against all the odds stacked up against us, at the end of the first day we had come back and won. It signalled the start of Steve Harmison's career change. Harmison went to the West Indies and came back the best fast bowler in the world. Vaughan grew as a captain, Thorpe was back and Flintoff would become the best all rounder in the world. It was the start of a great time for the England team. My only regret was that I wasn't five years younger and part of it. The next tour was to Bangladesh. I told David Graveney tongue in cheek I wasn't available. I also told him exactly what I thought about my non selection over the previous 10 years. I proved I could do it, I proved I could do it on flat pitches against the best players in the world. I had proved something to myself and that was far more important to me than anything else, full stop. Never would I sit there again and think 'would I be good enough to perform at the top level'? I knew I was good enough, and David Graveney finally knew I was good enough too. I kept telling him.

The party moved on to a top London restaurant that night. We had already been drinking for six hours at the ground after the match so you can imagine what state we were in. Butcher could hardly stand up and the rest of us weren't far behind. Flintoff was, as you can imagine, going along very well; it takes a lot to stop that man. Off to a nightclub, don't remember having to buy a drink all night and in bed by 4am. Bloody good night out! Rumour has it Freddie thought it would be a good idea to throw eggs at David Blaine that night; I think that went down well with most of England. My lasting memory of that night however was a conversation I had with Michael Vaughan. He told me he thought what I had done was remarkable, to come back after 10 years and perform the way I did. He trusted me ahead of all the other bowlers available to him. I was a little taken aback to say the least. What a lovely thing for someone to say. It came a little late in my career but nonetheless it was still pretty special.

# Implosion and Steve Rixon – A Disastrous Two Years

At the back end of the 2003 season Surrey County Cricket Club imploded. Nine trophies in seven years and the era had come to an end. If you look back at all the top clubs from the last 30 years you will see that no one has dominated for so long. Middlesex, Essex, Warwickshire and Gloucestershire have all had periods of success. It can't last forever. Players retire, lose form and teams change. It's how you deal with it that counts. We had a nightmare.

Our problem stemmed from the fact we had all grown old together. The younger players coming in hadn't really made enough of a mark. They wanted instant success, to play for England and win more trophies. But they didn't understand the work ethic needed to be successful. In the early part of our success we worked hard, we earned the right to win titles. It is easy to keep a winning side if you don't look to the future. If the side is winning why change it? Why upset the balance of the team to give a younger guy more experience, especially if a senior player is still performing well. We didn't quite get the balance right and would suffer in the long run.

# Martin Bicknell

In the game at Nottingham in 2003 we left out Graham Thorpe, Jon Batty, Ricki Clarke and Ian Salisbury. We had too many top players and couldn't keep them all happy anymore. The club also came under pressure financially. For many years the club had held back giving us more money by claiming we hadn't won anything. Now we had, and the club got themselves into a big financial hole trying to keep players happy. Success means players get paid more and with so many top players on big salaries someone had to go. The only player out of contract was Ian Ward. The club had to let one player go for financial reasons and unfortunately it was him. Scott Newman was knocking on the door and would be a good replacement in the long term, so it was seen as the easy option. The decision didn't help the mood in the dressing room either. It also didn't help Keith Medlycott.

Keith Medlycott, our coach at the time, had a difficult decision to make – who would follow Adam as captain? There weren't too many outstanding candidates. Medlycott had been perceived as very much Adam's number two, but now he had to take over and run the show. Senior players were starting to doubt whether he could do that and when the appointment of Jon Batty, a strange choice in everyone's eyes, was announced, what took place can only be described as a revolt. There were phone calls flying everywhere, players wanting the coach sacked, Batty removed and someone else appointed. Chaos reigned. During the whole process I really felt for both Medlycott and Batty, two top guys, but both in the wrong place at the wrong time. Keith's position became untenable and JB's position as captain had no backing in the team. We were now asking the man who kept wicket and opened the batting to captain a group of increasingly opinionated and difficult players. It was never going to work. Something needed to happen.

Something did happen; Medlycott was removed from his position. The club had no choice after some of the players said they would not stay if Medlycott was still coach, again, another awful situation. This whole fiasco could have been avoided; a little more communication could have placated the senior players and help smooth the transition between captains. The bottom line was that it was the wrong appointment and everyone bar Medlycott could see it. No one in their right mind could have kept wicket, opened the batting and captained the side, especially for Surrey. It cost Medlycott his job.

Medders actually came out to Spain to talk to both me and JB. We were on a golf tour at the time. I think he had already made up his mind who was going to be captain, but I threw a spanner in the works and said I would do the job for a year. I knew JB would have an impossible job, and I thought if I did it for a year JB could follow. I didn't want the job at all but I knew the problems he was about to face. I could have handled the senior players in the transition period we were about to face. But his mind was already made up. I think he wanted someone he could control; he had taken a bit of criticism about being in the background, behind Adam. Now he had to step forward and take more of a lead role. He didn't get the chance.

People will no doubt want to know my role in all this and where I stood on the issue. For the record I thought Medders was, and still is a great bloke. His record as a coach speaks for itself. He had great success in South Africa before coming back to Surrey. His partnership with Adam was tailor-made. Medders could sit behind Adam and let him be the dominant character. The only time Medders had to take sole control of the team was when Adam stayed behind in Australia when Ben died. In my opinion he struggled to lead the side when he should have been stamping his authority. Some senior players doubted he could play that role, and I was one of them. When the shit hit the fan at the end of 2003 I thought the reactions of some of our senior players was disgusting. I was divided in my thoughts. On one hand it might have been a good idea for both Adam and Medders to quit together. They had such a good partnership that working with someone else would never be the same again. On the other hand he deserved a chance to carry on and work with someone new because of what he had achieved and the success we had. As I said before, Medders' position became untenable very quickly and the club had to act. It wouldn't have happened if the situation had been handled better by all concerned. The way he left the club was very disappointing and he still doesn't talk to a few of the players he knew wanted him out.

The search for a new coach was on. My preference was for a coach who could come in and inject a bit of discipline into the side, a worker, who could get us back on track. With Jon Batty as captain we were going to need someone to be the disciplinarian and to take control. Someone was needed who could instil a better work ethic into the younger players and command the respect of the senior players. I happened to be in Sydney for the Rugby World Cup along with my good friend and Surrey's cricket chairman, Richard Thompson. We had one person in mind who came with a great CV – Steve Rixon. What had worked well for New Zealand and New South Wales should fit the bill for Surrey. We asked a few people, sought various opinions and it was all good. This man could do the job. David Gilbert, the ex-Surrey and now New South Wales supremo gave us permission to speak to Steve. I suppose we should have realised then that there was something not quite right. As it transpired, we learnt later that New South Wales were only too happy to see him leave. He had had major problems with some of the Aussies, including Steve Waugh, and they were looking to replace him anyway.

However, we were happy. I was in on the interview with Steve and he sounded like my kind of guy. I knew he faced a tough job though. The Surrey team, so dominant in the past few years, was in decline. Age was catching up with a few, injuries to key players meant we weren't quite the force we had been and in addition, an increasingly fractious dressing room, with a captain no one wanted, wasn't going to make his job any easier. We didn't mention any of that though. What we wanted was organisation, discipline and a good knowledge of the game at the highest level. He brought those qualities – or so we thought.

The 2004 season began with the usual optimism. The Batty saga had died down and we were all going to get behind him, unite and return to winning trophies, even though we all thought he was the wrong choice. Replacing the captain was not an option, we were told. Adam was now just a player. I'd had my little run in Test cricket and enjoyed it, but now it was Surrey business. Our first game, Oxford University at The Parks, gave us a fair indication of the problems the year would bring. Rixon, not a man to mince his words, told me and whomever else was listening that Ali Brown, admittedly not the prettiest of players, was a bit of a joker with the bat and that he didn't really rate him! Talk about labelling your players early on!

# Martin Bicknell

Alex Tudor, who struggled with many injuries over his career, also had a problem in this game, got injured and didn't bowl in the second innings. Rixon was all prepared to release him from his contract! He thought Alex was a faker and wanted to wash his hands of him there and then. The man had only been in the country six weeks! Another to be put out to grass was Alan Butcher. Alan, a very respected batting coach and someone all our batters had a lot of time for, was forced to take a back seat for a couple of weeks while Steve brought over his batting coach from New South Wales to 'have a look' at our batting line-up and point them in the right direction! After six weeks in the job Steve had certainly put his marker down, alienating one of our best batters, nearly sacking our quickest bowler and virtually making redundant the best batting coach in England. Well played Steve! The guy certainly knew how to make an impression.

I don't know what his agenda was. Obviously he wanted to stamp his authority on the team but you felt he was trying to do everything at once. He talked of a long-term plan for the club, but made rash decisions. Surely you need to take a little longer before rushing headlong into changing things?

On the field and into the season things certainly weren't going well. We lost in a C&G Trophy game to Ireland – yes – Ireland, a team with no internationals (that's unless you include Ireland itself as international) against our team, full of internationals. The night before the game the rain was lashing down and with no prospect of play we indulged in a couple of pints of Guinness. Well, quite a few pints actually; agreed, it was not very professional but it is the sort of thing that goes on from time to time when teams are away from home. It was a very funny night and good for morale. Needless to say Rixon knew nothing about it and didn't need to.

# BICKERS

Imagine our shock when we started at 12am the next day in brilliant sunshine! We lost the toss, batted, and scored 250. We should have got a few more, but it was still a good score. Due to more rain in the afternoon we didn't have to field so we got away with it. Early to bed, go out and win the game tomorrow – or so we thought. The next morning was cold, with the sort of horrible cross wind that all bowlers hate and we managed to serve up some dross with the ball and got soundly beaten. Throughout our bowling 'efforts' Rixon paced around the ground, shaking his head and muttering. If it hadn't been so important it would have been hilarious. It was embarrassing and we got the full Rixon blast – and rightly so. This was a team in freefall and things weren't going to get any better.

The guy I felt sorriest for was Jon Batty, struggling to impose himself on the team. Trying to open the batting and keep wicket was all proving too much for him. Again Rixon didn't really help by admitting he was going to look for a new captain when the season was over. But nor did the performances of the players. Adam should have retired the previous season. His heart wasn't in it and half way through the year Rixon told him he wasn't going to play in any more four-day matches. We still managed to get to the final of the Twenty20 competition, only to lose to Leicestershire. That was about the highlight of our season. I missed a large chunk of it with a tear in my groin. I came back into the side near the end of the season and we put together a good run to finish in a respectable position in the Championship. But it was a rubbish year.

By the last game of the season a lot of the players had had enough, Rixon had made himself so unpopular in the course of the year that many of the players hoped he would go. We were playing Sussex with nothing riding on the game. As so often happens in these games, punctuality and discipline weren't high on everyone's agenda. Even Mark Ramprakash turned up late one morning! Rixon blew his top and sulked for most of the match. It was childish – but not something that wouldn't happen again as things deteriorated between players and management.

One of the only bright spots in my year was getting to a thousand first-class wickets. For quite a while it had been on my mind and during the Kent game I got to the magic number. Mathew Dennington nicked one through to Jon Batty in a replica dismissal to my first first-class wicket 18 years ago. I was so relieved to finally get there. It was a special moment. To me, a thousand first-class wickets raise you to another level. Only about 15 other Surrey players have got to that mark and only a couple in the last 30 years. I was a very proud man to join that elite crowd.

Next year we would have Mark Butcher as captain; Jon Batty was stood down. Rixon had another year on his contract and things had to improve. Off the field things had deteriorated between Loraine and me and we decided to split. It had been coming for quite a while now and people who knew us weren't that surprised. Being a professional cricketer can be very glamorous at times. Nice cars, good wages and a nice lifestyle. What isn't mentioned is the fact you can spend every other week away from home and your family can come second. When I met Loraine she understood what life would be like with me as a cricketer. But over the period of our relationship she became more independent, happy to do her own thing. We had growing issues that were just getting bigger and bigger. The only solution was to separate. The priority now was the children. We had to tell them I was moving out. I was dreading it but they took it brilliantly. I spent so much time away from them playing cricket that it wasn't a massive issue for them. My brother had also recently split from his wife so we had plenty to talk about.

I moved into a flat in Guildford. It wasn't the nice five-bedroomed house we had in Lightwater but it would do for the time being. With a Testimonial on the horizon I would be able to buy something for myself eventually.

The start of the 2005 season should have been a new beginning. A new year always brings hope, but our season never got going. Mark Butcher damaged his wrist and required surgery, robbing us of our captain for most of the year. What should have been a routine operation turned into a nightmare few months of problem after problem on his slow road to recovery. Mark Ramprakash took over the captaincy for what should have been a month, but which turned into four. Mark had captained Middlesex for a period before he came to Surrey, but grew very frustrated with his time in charge there. Mark is a complex character. Difficult to read sometimes and quite volatile, he found it very hard to understand bowlers' mentality as he had never been a bowler. He also found it difficult to understand why cricketers didn't work as hard as they could on their games. I have known Mark for a very long time. Throughout our time playing against each other I always admired his ability but never really got to know him that well. When he came to Surrey we knew we had signed an outstanding player, but we were all a little concerned as to how he would find our dressing room and its humour. We had formed a very close-knit unit and the thought of bringing in a sometimes volatile outsider was a concern. However his quality with the bat and the sheer weight of runs he scored for us soon put any potential problems to rest. True, when he gets out, you don't want to be within earshot of the dressing room, but that is just the guy – passionate about his cricket and with such a desire to do well.

Ramprakash was very much a pro-Rixon man, and the respect was mutual. Rixon often brought up Ramps' name when discussing what the club needed to do more of – and that was work harder. This was a fair point which I do not dispute. As someone who honed his art over countless hours in the nets I agree totally. The problem lies in the fact that in a squad of 22 players everyone is different and that to be a good coach and captain you have to handle everyone differently. Sometimes to get the best out of players, you have to treat them with understanding and realise they are not all just robots, but for some people this approach is a real challenge. There was too much inflexibility within our management and that led to conflict which festered over the season. Rixon wanted to play the game his way – the Australian way – win at all costs, draws mean nothing. Well, that approach doesn't work in our system. You do get rewarded for drawing games in this country. Obviously it is better to win, but if you can't, the last thing you do is offer that chance to the opposition. As players, we knew how to win Championships and that meant not giving the opposition so much as a sniff of victory. Even Ramps clashed with Rixon over that.

There were a couple of instances of this. At Birmingham against Warwickshire we were on the wrong end of a match and fighting hard to save the game. At lunch on the last day we were 120 in front with only two wickets down. Rixon made it very clear we should be thinking about setting them a target. All the players disagreed. We thought we should save the game that we had worked so hard to get back into and carry on batting to the end. There was too much discussion going on and we lost our focus for the afternoon session. We couldn't decide whether to stick or twist and got bowled out cheaply and lost the game. It wasn't the first time or the last that there was a conflict of opinion.

At Tunbridge Wells against Kent, we had been set over 400 runs to win. All day it looked as if we could win the game until we lost a couple of wickets and the chase was out of our reach. Had we carried on our unrealistic pursuit of victory and lost the game we would have given Kent, one of our rivals, an undeserved win. Ramps called off the chase, we drew the game and got the points for a draw. Rixon called a meeting at the end of the game and it all kicked off. The two of them ended up in a slanging match across the dressing room for all the players to hear and they both stormed off to the car park and drove home. All this was happening at the same time as the ball tampering affair. It was fast becoming a season to forget.

I think the event that brought everything to a head was the game at Bristol against Gloucestershire. We still had ambition to win the title and we knew this was a game we had to win. Gloucestershire were now a poor side and along with Glamorgan that year were the whipping boys of the division. The only problem we anticipated was the pitch – always slow and low at Bristol – and we weren't to be disappointed. We won the toss, batted and declared just before lunch on the second day with our score over 600. Everyone had scored runs, but we knew the hard work was just starting. Bowling out Gloucester twice on this wicket, even with our recently signed overseas player, Harbhajan Singh, was going to be very tough – and so it proved. It took us until just after tea on the fourth day to do it, leaving us too many runs to chase to win the game. Still it was a mighty fine effort in very hot conditions and on an unresponsive wicket to get so close, a fact overlooked by our coach, who was once again sulking!

At the start of the third day of the match all the bowlers were taken to the pool for a gentle loosen up for the day ahead and to get rid of yesterday's stiffness. With breakfast running a little late and a fair journey to the ground, this meant we got onto the field for warm-ups five minutes late. Rixon was standing on the outfield as we arrived and exploded, even though we had legitimate reasons for being late. This was the last straw for Azhar Mahmood, our other overseas player, who gave it straight back to him with both barrels. This was totally out of character for Azhar, normally the most placid of people, but he, like everyone else, had had enough. Rixon's response? To not talk to anyone for the rest of the match! Not even a 'well done' for what was a very good effort in the conditions. He sulked for two days, got in his car at the end of the game and left. The writing was on the wall and at the end of the season there was mutual agreement for him to end his stay in England.

The season went rapidly downhill from that point. Lots of injuries and repeated failure to win games meant we got relegated, along with Glamorgan and Gloucestershire. It was my least enjoyable season in professional cricket. The dressing room was now split right down the middle. On one side you had the young guys, treating every away trip like party time, not taking their cricket seriously enough – and on the other, the senior players, resenting this attitude but not doing anything to try and change it. It was almost as though everyone had lost interest in the season and couldn't wait for it to end. At several points I considered calling it a day but the thought of Rixon leaving kept me going and the chance to make a fresh start was an opportunity I didn't want to miss. Injuries were now playing too big a part in my cricket. I missed the last six weeks of the season with a torn Achilles, but if I am honest I didn't miss the cricket. The atmosphere around the team was horrible. I was glad to be out of it. I knew my career was on the downhill stretch, but with the Testimonial year coming up I knew I had to give it one last shot and play my part in turning the club around.

The saving grace of the season came in England's triumph over Australia in The Ashes. It also stopped Rixon from being so smug over another Aussie triumph. I have witnessed far too many drubbings over the years not to have enjoyed this result. All through the summer we had gripping entertainment. I sat and watched the Fourth Test from Trent Bridge in my flat, feeling sick as we chased the runs. Counting them down felt like I was actually playing in the game. But the sense of relief when Ashley Giles hit the winning runs was immense. It set it up perfectly for the last Test at The Oval. I went every day, hoping and praying for rain, bad light, lightning, whatever else could stop the match. After years of losing to these guys, clutching defeat from the jaws of victory would have been too much to bear. The final day and I sat myself on the Exec balcony at The Oval with Barry Kitcherside, and with his help managed to get through several pints of Pimm's. Anything to take our minds off the game. I hadn't had so much that I didn't notice the most extraordinary performance by Kevin Pietersen. Pietersen might not be everyone's cup of tea but he is one of the few people I would pay to go and watch. As the runs flowed, so did the alcohol. We celebrated long and hard but probably not quite as hard as Freddie.

By this time I had met Jacqui and she was very much part of my life. I had been separated for five months and with almost perfect timing she bumped into me in Guildford. We had an instant rapport and things grew between us really quickly. I was also fortunate that the kids took to her immediately as well. She is an amazing woman, I am lucky to have her in my life.

Of course none of what happened over the two years was Rixon's fault! In a scathing attack on county cricket he called it a 'cesspool of mediocrity' amongst other things. Even after this interview, he still managed to turn up to Surrey's end of season awards night. By this stage not many of the players had a lot of time for him. The club's decision to replace him with Alan Butcher brought a huge sigh of relief around the club.

For all his faults I agreed with a lot of what Rixon was trying to do: integrate young players into the team, a better work ethic, and improved organisation. He just didn't get on with many people. John Buchanan faced similar problems at Middlesex. The approach of an Australian coach doesn't fit that well into our system. Whose fault is it? Is it ours? Do we have a soft culture where our players are mollycoddled? The Australian way is very much orientated to hard cricket and tough characters where the weak fall away. I guess that approach is OK when you only have six state teams and you can discard the weak players. However, in England, dealing with 24 players on your staff can be a bit like babysitting at times. The two cultures are very different and I don't think Rixon ever got that.

# The End is Nigh

I knew my time at the club was coming to an end. 2006 was always going to be my last year. A testimonial was awarded for my 21 years at the club. It was a nice gesture by the club and, with my divorce it was much needed! After my split with Loraine I had met Jacqui and by now we were living together. My kids had coped brilliantly with the changes in their lives, better than I had! Divorce is a very painful time in anyone's life; you wouldn't wish it on your worst enemy.

We started our 2006 season with a pre-season tour of India. Both my Achilles were giving me problems. I could hardly walk. Some mornings the pain was so bad – old age was definitely creeping up on me. I had missed the back end of 2005 with a torn Achilles, but I was determined to be part of the new-look Surrey however much I was struggling with niggling injuries. To be honest I was getting more pain through the divorce. Loraine was taking the kids and moving away from me. No longer would they be just down the road so I could see them whenever I wanted. Now it was going to be alternate weekends only. I was devastated. My kids obviously mean everything to me and this was the last straw. We were also having the usual arguments about money; the solicitors were getting in the way and it wasn't being dealt with very well. Jacqui was also having problems with her son, Tony. Tony was going through a hard time, finding life a struggle and it was affecting all of us. Me coming into the house as an outsider didn't really help things between him and his Mum. I wanted to be there for them both but most of the time I was just getting in the way. This created conflict between us at times, and neither of us handled it very well. Fortunately things have now improved between us. At the time however, Jacqui was alone as I was away, and she wasn't coping well at all. I was concerned for her but equally I felt I needed a shoulder to cry on myself. It all got too much for me; I couldn't keep it all in. All the build up and frustration came to a point one morning in India and I broke down. I was fortunate that I had people around me who knew exactly what I was going through and could talk about it. Unless you have been through that emotional pain it is very hard to describe. At Surrey, we had lots of broken marriages. I think it goes with the job. Tim Laskey, my former trainer once said to me 'a physical pain you can deal with, but emotional pain is by far the worst'. He got it spot on.

Out on the pitch I was going OK. It was hard work but pre-season had gone pretty well and I was really looking forward to giving it one last crack. However, the dreaded injury curse struck and a thigh problem ruled me out for a couple of weeks. Having missed the first couple of weeks of the season I was eager to get back into the side. The team had started well. We were in the Second Division for the first time and were desperate to get back into the big league. I came back too early and did it again. Being injured is the bane of all professional sportsmen. I always found the first day of the injury the worst, waiting for the diagnosis, learning how long you are going to be out for, and getting your rehab plan from the physio. The older you get the worse it is. Injuries take that bit longer to heal, getting fit again takes longer and the words 'wear and tear' just mean your body is gradually falling apart. Get past 30 and if you are a sportsman you are a time bomb waiting to go off. It wasn't until 31st May that I managed to get myself fit enough to play. I missed six weeks for an injury that should have taken two at the most.

Essex were the visitors at Whitgift School and I was back in. Azhar Mahmood and Mo Akram took the new ball and I was first change. How times change. I was nervous as hell. Running into bowl I felt pressure for the first time in ages. I wasn't too sure how much Mark and Alan Butcher wanted me in the side. I think they really wanted to blood new players. The two Pakistanis were going well and in Salisbury and Doshi we had two spinners who were taking loads of wickets. I didn't feel that wanted. After the end of the first day I felt pretty low. The divorce was really getting me down and I hadn't bowled that well. I wanted to call it a day, to retire there and then. I had had enough. We batted on the second day so I had a good chat with Alan Butcher. I told him I wasn't prepared to play on in this frame of mind. I had lost the competitive edge. The divorce and injuries were taking the wind out of my sails. Alan was good about the whole thing and we agreed to assess things over the next couple of weeks.

Later that second day I came into bat. We were going pretty well but when I came in I wasn't ready for what came at me. Ronnie Irani got into me from the moment I took guard and he didn't stop. I let it go for a while, thinking he would have his little rant and then back down a bit. But he didn't and it got to the point where I felt myself bubbling up. Normally a batsman just blocks it out and ignores it. I wasn't ready to do that. I had enough other worries without him giving me more grief. I stopped the bowler at the end of his run-up and took off towards him. I gave it to him with both barrels. He had picked the wrong guy that day. The umpires stepped in before things escalated; I was ready for a fight.

Irani and Surrey also have some history, and this didn't help. In a floodlit game at Chelmsford a couple of years earlier, we had needed to play to win the game and the league. It had rained and the outfield was a bit damp. It drizzled a bit and then stopped and the last inspection took place. Bearing in mind there was a full house for this game you would have thought Irani would want to play for all the people who had paid good money at his home ground. Not a bit of it. He whinged so much the umpires called the game off. Ronnie went home smiling. The very next year we were back at Chelmsford for a Twenty20 game under lights, on Sky TV. This time the situation was reversed. Essex were desperate to play so they could qualify for the quarter-finals. It was raining hard with not much chance of playing. The umpires kept inspecting and to our total disbelief they said the game would start, in the rain. It was a farce. Ronnie, being interviewed before the start of the game said "we are in the entertainment industry and have a duty to our paying public to play". Honestly, the garbage that came out of his mouth. It ended up being a five-over game in some of the worst weather you have ever seen. Essex won and once again, Irani got what he wanted. Ali Brown who captained Surrey in that game got stuck into Ronnie on Sky at the end of the game. As I said, Surrey and Ronnie don't see eye to eye.

The little spat at Whitgift with Ronnie got me going. It reignited my competitive streak. Second innings I bowled a great spell and we ended up winning the game. Although I didn't take any wickets I felt better about myself, felt part of the team again. Having missed the last six games of the previous season and the first six of this one, I just needed to fire up. It felt like I had missed a whole year. New players had come in and Surrey were once again moving in the right direction. I really wanted to play my part.

After beating Essex so convincingly we then destroyed Leicester at The Oval. Leicester showed up the Second Division for what it was. The best teams are in the First Division. There is no argument about that. Some of the teams in the Second Division were really poor. We were dominating this league now and promotion was a near certainty.

Next up were Somerset at Bath. After playing a couple of games in a row I felt part of the team again. There would only be another two games to play before the month break for the Twenty20 cricket started. As I wasn't playing any one-day cricket I thought "If I can play these two games I could have a break". I was still struggling with niggling injury problems that wouldn't go away. Every day was hard work. After a while it just grinds you down. In all honesty I was looking forward to retirement.

We arrived at Bath on the morning of the match. The first thing I like to do is go and have a look at the wicket. It was green and damp, perfect for seam bowling, perfect for my bowling. We won the toss, bowled first and the ball seamed and swung everywhere. It was hard to bowl a straight ball, it moved around so much. At this stage of my career I really needed some help from the pitch but this was ridiculous. Mo Akram and I bowled well, so well in fact that we bowled for much of the day. I ended up bowling 27 overs and taking five wickets. The fifth one, Andrew Caddick, was my one-thousandth Championship wicket. I didn't know it at the time but it was also my last ever wicket for Surrey.

# Martin Bicknell

The 27 overs in a day did for me. I woke next morning and could not get out of bed. Not only was I stiff and sore, but I was exhausted as well. Somerset were nine wickets down and still batting, so I had to open the bowling again. I went through all the warm-ups, the stretching and tried to get myself ready. It just wasn't happening. I know I am not the quickest bowler in the world and at the age of 37 I had lost a yard or two. But that first over of the second day had to be one of the slowest I have ever delivered. I was gone, shot to pieces, nothing left in the tank. In the second innings I gave it everything I had but didn't really look like taking a wicket. Gone was the lithe teenager who could bowl all day, then do it again the next. That body had been replaced by some clapped out old pensioner's version. God, I felt old! We did win the game however, and being out there as the winning runs were hit gave me great satisfaction, especially as they came off Andrew Caddick. However, there wasn't too much more I could take. Once you have lost the hunger and the desire you may as well pack up and I wasn't that far off. The fat lady was clearing her throat.

The game at Swansea against Glamorgan, my fourth game in four weeks, was my last for the club. It wasn't meant to be that way but history will tell you it was. Nothing really exciting happened. I didn't take a wicket, though I scored a good 50, but the game petered out into a draw. I felt I had bowled OK. With a month off coming up I gave it all that I had. It just wasn't good enough anymore. I left the ground on the evening of the fourth day with that month off to look forward to before the next game at Northants.

The month off gave me time to work on the Testimonial, play some golf, see the kids and play the odd game for the second team and

# BICKERS

Guildford. My Guildford connection was and is still very strong. The captain, Tim Walter, and I go back to the days when I joined the club as a 12-year-old. I still have many friends down there and feel a real affinity with the club. It was ironic that my last ever game for Surrey would be there. One of my final games was for Guildford, during the Twenty20 break. I really enjoyed coming back to help the team out, catch up with a few mates and play some cricket. We were playing Reigate Priory who were the dominant side in the Division. We batted first and I went in number four. I thought I would have a little look at the bowling and then score a nice 50. I played forward to the leg spinner and gloved a catch to silly point, for 0. After posting a smallish score I planned to come out, bowl a few overs and take a couple of wickets. I got smashed all over the ground; even the Reigate Priory opener chirped me at one point. I am sure some of the players were asking if this was the same player who played for England. I couldn't even perform for Guildford any more, it was definitely time to retire.

The Twenty20 came and went. Surrey once again made it to finals day, only to get knocked out by Notts in the semi-finals. Surrey's next four-day game was at Northampton. We practised the day before and after the break I was really looking forward to playing again. The games I played in the month off may not have always gone to plan but I was preparing myself for the final push. But it wasn't to be. The morning of the game I woke with a really stiff back. I just couldn't get going; I had to make a decision about playing. Knowing I couldn't operate at less than 100% I sat the game out. We went on to win the game comfortably. Next stop Guildford, and Somerset.

# Martin Bicknell

All year I had looked at the fixture list and the game that really stood out for me was Somerset at Guildford. I so wanted to play in the game. It would mean so much to me to have one final game on a ground where I had grown up, learnt my trade, and have so many friends. Anil Kumble had joined the staff for the second half of the year and I knew the Butchers were contemplating playing three spinners. If this happened I probably wouldn't play. I went to the ground the day before for a fitness test with Geoff Arnold and looked at the wicket. I couldn't see too much reason to play three spinners so I thought I would play. I bowled for 40 minutes with no problem, declared myself fit and went home. Throughout the afternoon I was restless, I wanted to know if I was playing. I rang Alan Butcher in the evening at home and he said it would be between me and third spinner. It didn't help me sleep. I had built up this match so much in my head. It had got to the point that if someone had said this will be your last ever game and then you will retire, I would have accepted it.

On the morning of the game I got to the ground around 9.15am. The first person I saw was Alan Butcher. "You won't be playing" were the first words I heard. I was gutted to say the least. I was even more gutted when he said they would be playing Neil Saker, a seamer, in my place. It wasn't between me and the other spinner at all. They had decided to play the same team that won at Northampton. Now, I don't have a problem when it comes to selection issues. For what it's worth, it was perhaps the right decision for the future of the club. What I did have an issue with was the way it was all handled. I didn't need to go for a fitness test, and I certainly didn't need to go to the ground on the morning of the game if I wasn't ever going to play. I felt I deserved a little better than that.

# BICKERS

The next series of events were even worse. After a couple of days at the ground watching, Alan and I went for a walk around the boundary. He apologised for the way things had been handled, blamed a lack of communication between him and Mark, the captain. He asked me if I fancied playing in the one-day game on the Sunday. I jumped at the chance. He knew how much playing at the club meant to me and I thought it was a great gesture. I hadn't played a lot of one-day cricket recently so I had to get my kit down from The Oval. The plan was I would play for Guildford on the Saturday, to get some more match practice, and then Surrey on the Sunday. It didn't quite work out like that. During the Saturday afternoon I got a call from Alan saying they weren't going play me after all. They were going to keep the same side from the last one-day game. I was now slightly more than annoyed. Why do that to me? I think Alan Butcher has done a great job with Surrey and I am really happy for him after years as the number two. But at this point in time he wasn't my favourite bloke in the world.

I went to the ground on the Sunday anyway. It was fairly painful watching the guys warm up on the outfield before the game, knowing my last chance to play at Guildford had gone. I couldn't even look Alan Butcher in the eye I was that disappointed. I knew the writing was on the wall and I didn't see myself playing too much more anyway. Alan had said as much in our chat during the week. He did say to keep playing if I could, because "you never know when you might be needed". After 21 years it wasn't really what I wanted to hear.

That was enough for me; the life had been sucked out of my body. I now hated getting up in the mornings to play, the soreness, the aching and the pain were really getting to me now. I agreed to play one more game. Ironically it was back at Guildford for the second team against Durham. I wasn't looking forward to it to be honest. There wasn't much adrenaline left in the body and although I bowled pretty well and scored some runs, the fight had left my body. I woke on the last day of the game and said 'enough is enough'. That day would be my last day's cricket for Surrey County Cricket Club. I had been talking it over with Jacqui for a while. She saw how much effort it was taking to play and the struggle it involved. There was no option really; it was all over for me now. I got to the ground and did the warm-ups. I was again struggling with a sore back. I had a think about it and said, I just can't do it. I didn't even get on to the field.

I spoke to Nadeem Shahid, coach of the second team and told him my decision. I phoned Alan Butcher as well. I said that I would come into the ground the next day and tell the lads myself. There was still six weeks of the season left but for me it was over. It felt like a huge weight off my shoulders. I didn't have to bowl anymore; I didn't have to put my body through any more pain. It was the right time to call it a day. No longer would I scan the averages to see where I stood; no longer would I worry about to whom I was going to bowl, and no longer would I wear the brown cap on the field of play. It was well and truly over.

I went to The Oval the next day and watched the afternoon session from the dressing room. I didn't tell any of the lads beforehand what I had decided to do. At the end of the day's play Alan said that I had something to say. I started my little speech about retiring but the words barely came out. I managed to utter something but it didn't make any sense. The enormity of the curtain coming down on my career was too much. I didn't think it would affect me like that but I guess I am a bit of a softie at heart. We sat around for ages afterwards and shared a few drinks and stories of how good I used to be!

News spread pretty fast. I did a couple of interviews and some of the newspapers did nice pieces on me. The overriding opinion was still that I should have played more for my country and in truth they are probably right. However, I don't lose any sleep over it. I played for England; a lot of good players didn't, including my brother. I would happily give him one of my four Test caps. I have great memories of that day at The Oval, the Sunday where I helped England win a Test match. The celebrations that followed, the feeling that I was good enough to wear the three lions on my shirt and an acceptance by others that maybe they were wrong when it came to my non selection. That was enough for me.

It is probably fair to say that I have been good for Surrey and Surrey have definitely been good for me. They had the best years of my life, although my body suffered more than most. I managed to clock up 11 operations in the 21 years I was at the club. Both Achilles, knees, wrist, shoulder, hamstring, rib, ankle and my nose twice. I had a pretty good relationship with a number of surgeons and specialists. I had many cortisone injections, played when I shouldn't have done and took more pain killers than I care to mention. If they ever outlawed those lovely painkilling pink brufen tablets, most bowlers' careers would be over. I loved it all though. Of course some days really were grim, but the next morning would always bring new optimism.

I have nothing but good to say about Surrey County Cricket Club. Since the age of 10 I have represented Surrey for a total of 28 seasons. We have been through highs and lows, tragedy and triumph and throughout it all I have never wanted to play for any other side. I have a passion for the club so that even now I follow every ball to see how they are getting on. I sit on the General Committee, the Cricket Committee and the Surrey Cricket Review Group. It is in my blood and I can't see that changing.

I was lucky enough to have won many awards, trophies and titles. I have part of the new stand named after me, and I have a painting of me hanging in the Long Room. I took over 1500 wickets in all cricket and scored over 8000 runs. But the memories aren't of me as an individual. The images I will keep with me are the team ones. Winning the Sunday League in 1996, my first team trophy. The two winning Lord's finals, the celebrations and the nights out afterwards. Winning the County Championship in 1999 for the first time in 28 years, defending it, and then winning it again in 2002. These are the things that mean more to me than individual triumphs.

Without me Surrey went on to win the Second Division title. I was really happy for the team and both the Butchers. They had put a lot of things right from the previous regime and now Surrey would be back in the First Division, where they belong. The 2007 season would start without a Bicknell in sight. Darren had decided to retire as well, bringing an end to his fantastic career. We both finished on our own terms, and that was important.

# Ball Tampering

OK. Let's dispel a few myths. Ball tampering has been around for a long time, well before it was discovered by the latest generation of cricketers and it will carry on, in one form or another, so long as cricket is played. So, is it cheating or gamesmanship?

The dictionary tells us that cricket balls are made from a core of cork, layered with tightly wound string and covered by a leather case with a slightly raised sewn seam. The covering is constructed of four pieces of leather, shaped similar to the peel of a quartered orange, but one hemisphere is rotated by 90 degrees with respect to the other. The "equator" of the ball is stitched with string to form the seam, with a total of six rows of stitches. The remaining two joins between the leather pieces are left unstitched.

Weighing around 5.75 ounces and nine inches in circumference, the cricket ball is a lethal weapon in the hands of a fast bowler. It is also a delicately made object that has to sustain severe wear and tear from hard surfaces – and the bat – over the 80 overs, or more of its life. During an extended period of play, the ball's surface wears down and becomes rough. This affects the aerodynamics of the flight of the ball, which can be affected by a number of factors, including the bowler's action. The movement of the air around the ball is crucial to its flight when it leaves the bowler's hand. More of this later.

Bowlers are allowed to polish the ball – by rubbing it on their trousers, once having applied saliva or sweat onto the surface. Usually they will only polish one side in order to create aerodynamic 'swing'. The way the ball is held and gripped with the fingers will also influence the flight of the ball. The seam can also be used to produce different trajectories, with the technique known as swing bowling, or to produce sideways movement as the ball bounces off the pitch – hence the term seam bowling.

Since the condition of the cricket ball is crucial to the amount of movement through the air, the laws governing what players may and may not do to it are specific and rigorously enforced by umpires. They cannot rub anything apart from saliva or sweat onto the ball, rub it on the ground, scuff it, or tamper with it using their fingernails. Most importantly, a bowler must not pick at, or lift the seam of the ball in any area, particularly where it is unstitched.

A new cricket ball is harder than a worn one and is preferred by fast bowlers because of the speed and bounce they can get off the pitch. At the same time, uneven wear on older balls may also make reverse swing possible, and this art is something faster bowlers have exploited successfully over the past 30 years. Despite the strict application of the rules by umpires, it can be tempting for players to accelerate the deterioration of the ball to their advantage, or to put it another way, bend the rules in their favour.

There have been a handful of incidents of so-called ball tampering at the highest levels of cricket, involving players such as the Pakistani fast bowler Waqar Younis and former England captain Mike Atherton. The most recent was in 2006 in a Test series here in England against Pakistan. A decision taken by umpires Darrell Hare and Billy Doctrove ultimately led to the Fourth Test between England and Pakistan at The Oval being brought to a premature end. The Pakistan players were so upset at a five-run penalty imposed by Hare and Doctrove during the afternoon's play that they failed to take the field promptly after the tea interval. The match was awarded to England by forfeit. The row had flared when the Pakistani captain, Imzaman ul-haq, was accused by Darrell Hare of altering the condition of the ball.

A subsequent inspection by the former Middlesex and Durham seam bowler, Simon Hughes, concluded the ball was in "pretty good condition." He reported that there were a number of small abrasions on the rough side, fairly typical of normal wear and tear on a deteriorating Test pitch. He said later in *The Daily Telegraph*: "The only thing that looked slightly suspicious was a number of slightly curved striations concentrated on one area. I concluded that those could have been man-made scratches but there was no way I could be sure. There was no hard evidence of ball-tampering." At a later hearing Imzaman ul-haq was cleared of altering the condition of the ball.

I have a robust view of ball tampering. I regard it as legitimate gamesmanship and it can amount to an art form. Blatant scratching of one side is, quite rightly, looked upon as unfair. But manipulating the ball; keeping one side dry and letting the other side rough up, is not cheating. There must always be a line you cannot step over, but operating just either side of it is part of the game.

So what constitutes ball tampering? Scratching the ball? Lifting the quarter seam? Picking the seam? Applying some form of substance on the ball? Any bowler who tells you he has not tampered with the ball is probably lying. So where do we draw the line between cheating and gamesmanship? It does not just apply to bowlers in cricket. A batsman can nick the ball to the keeper, stand his ground knowing he is out and thus cheat on the other team. It is accepted as part of the game. The fielding side can appeal for a decision knowing the batsman is not out; again it is a form of cheating.

Gamesmanship is alive and well in all sports. Let us take football for example. How many forwards go to ground in the penalty area at the slightest touch from a defender? The attacker will anticipate a tackle is coming, push the ball a bit further and instead of jumping the tackle he will leave his leg out in the hope of a slight contact. The referee whistles for a penalty. Job done!

Why is it that we only point the finger at foreigners? I remember vividly watching Gary Lineker bearing down on goal in a match against Cameroon in the World Cup of some years ago. He hardly came into contact with the defender, but hit the ground as though he'd been shot and won a penalty. We turned a blind eye to his cheating because Gary Lineker was one of ours. He was doing it for England and the game was vital to England's progress in the competition.

In cricket, Pakistan have had to put up with allegations of cheating through ball tampering for a long time from the rest of the world. I have sympathy for them. They play, for the most part, on hard, abrasive and slow wickets that tend to favour the batsman. However, sub-continental wickets lend themselves to reverse swing bowling. Consequently, the

# BICKERS

Pakistanis in particular have learned to exploit the way the ball deteriorates and they try to turn it to their advantage. They do it cleverly and were the first to develop the art of reverse swing.

As I mentioned earlier, getting the ball to reverse swing is largely a question of aerodynamics. In simple terms, the Pakistani bowlers worked out that the ball will only change its flight path as it travels towards the batsman when the air around the surface of the ball is moving at different speeds. Once it leaves the bowler's hand, the ball pushes air to the side as it travels forward. Why? Because the air must go somewhere. These are the laws of physics. Why do aeroplanes take off or why do yachts go forward into the wind?

The opposite side to the polished surface is left to roughen up under the normal wear and tear of the game. Air likes smooth surfaces and so it flows more quickly around that half. Suction occurs and the ball moves left or right in its flight. Eventually the ball gets very old and then the air changes its preference. The rough side starts to gather the air and slow it down. If you keep the other side well polished and slightly heavier, then that is when reverse swing comes into play. So, without changing the position of the seam, the ball begins to swing in the opposite direction in what we call "reverse" swing. The seam hasn't changed, but the air has changed its preference for the surface of the ball. Confused? I believe cricket involves many complex and intricate factors, including mind games that we just don't encounter in other outdoor sports. The art of ball tampering plays an important part in cricket's elevation to something more than just a sport.

The ball doesn't have to be 45 or more overs old before it will reverse swing. I have seen a newish ball around 10 overs old start to do it. Even in 20-over cricket Surrey managed to get the ball to 'reverse'.

Professional cricketers in the modern era have become more scientific in their application to the game. Also the days have gone when a bowler could scratch the ball openly and not worry about the umpire being too vigilant. Nowadays a player has to look after the rough side of the ball in a way that is undetectable. He or she must make sure the natural scuff marks on an ageing ball stay rough and dry. It is easy to do and hard to detect. Is it gamesmanship or cheating? Have I been involved? Of course I have.

You don't have to be a 90mph-plus bowler in order to be effective with a reverse swinging ball, although if it is delivered at that speed it can have a damaging and disconcerting effect upon the confidence of a batting line-up. One of the best exponents of reverse swing was the Australian Adam Hollioake, with whom I played at Surrey and who bowled at slightly more than 70mph. When Adam got it right, he caused major problems for batsmen coming in at the end of a one-day game and his contribution to Surrey's success during his era was immense. Batsmen feared him.

Bowlers of seam and spin, fast, medium and slow, are always looking for ways to get the upper hand on the batsman. They would love the ball to swing naturally all of the time, but patience – and waiting for the moment – is essential. Unobtrusively they keep the rough side dry and scuff the odd mark on the ball in the hope that the ball starts to swing even more. I would challenge any top-class bowler who hasn't done that to stand up!

As an example let us look again at the Fourth Test at The Oval in 2006 when England won because Pakistan forfeited the match. Could that infamous episode have been avoided? I am sure it could, and it was certainly bad for international cricket.

Darryl Hare had been appointed as an umpire for nine out of Pakistan's 17 previous Tests. Pakistan had a problem with Hare, who has resolute and strict views on what he sees as illegal ball tampering. This was well known, yet the ICC failed to avoid the potential time bomb by appointing Hare, rather than someone else, to umpire at The Oval. In hindsight, the entire episode was badly handled. Somehow, we managed to get to the stage where a Test was abandoned on the flimsy evidence that the ball may have been scuffed in a few areas. Common sense should have prevailed. The problem that arose in that match on that day could have been addressed in a different way.

The Pakistan Cricket Board were adamant the entire incident could have been avoided if the ICC had accepted their earlier request that Darryl Hare should not be an umpire in matches involving their side. PCB chairman Shaharyar Khan is reported as saying: "We told them we had a problem with his attitude, so why post him to four successive series. It was a time bomb waiting to go off and it went off."

I do not want to blame Darryl Hare for what went wrong with the 2006 Test Series. However, it is significant that when Sri Lanka had a problem with him in 1995, he was not posted to a Sri Lanka match for eight years. The ICC may hold the view that no country should have the right to choose the umpires who will be appointed for a particular match. Were they guilty of stunning obstinacy that year? I think so.

I believe it is now time for the law on ball tampering to be reviewed and overhauled. Visual guesswork – judging whether a ball has been tampered with – should not be the only way to ensure fair play when television evidence to support any judgement is available.

Reverse swing is an exciting thing to watch – so why not encourage it? Flat wickets and non-swinging cricket balls, can lead to dull cricket. Many Test matches played on the Indian sub-continent are destined to be tedious draws after the first day, because it is so difficult to get batsmen out. Pakistan has shown we should encourage the unorthodox skill of the bowler to come through. After all, any bowler's reverse swing has to be delivered with a high amount of skill if it is going to be effective.

Wasim Akram, and the 'Burewala Express', Waqar Younis, both of Pakistan, were literally unplayable when the ball was reverse swinging and they were brilliant to watch. They spearheaded the bowling regularly for Pakistan in the early to mid-Nineties and Waqar's most recognised delivery was the inswinging yorker. He once took seven wickets for 76 runs in a Test match and he took his first 50 Test wickets in just 10 matches.

During the Pakistan-England Test Series in 1992, British journalists were deeply suspicious of the results the Pakistani bowlers were getting from reverse swing. Allegations of illegal ball tampering were being murmured, probably because English bowlers had not by then perfected the technique of ball tampering to the same degree.

Waqar, who became a good friend of mine when he played at Surrey, has subsequently gone down in the annals of Test cricket, with Alan Donald and Glenn McGrath, as the most deadly of fast bowlers in the 1900s. While other bowlers played much of their cricket on fast bouncy wickets, Waqar had to deal more often with slower sub-continental wickets. Yet he still took wickets through individual brilliance. In all my years of playing cricket, I have never seen anyone so destructive and so talented. He was great to watch, great to play with and probably taught more English bowlers the art of reverse swing than many of us would be prepared to admit.

Some of the stories about ball tampering have now drifted into legend. In an English county fixture we even had an episode in a game between Glamorgan and Gloucestershire where Steve Kirby was accused of picking up the ball in a car park, after the ball had been hit for six and rubbing it on the gravel to rough one side of it up. The Glamorgan coach at the time, John Derrick, claimed he saw this happen and reported it to the ECB. Kirby got away with those allegations, on the basis they were hearsay.

I remember a game against Sussex at Hove one year when the issue flared up again. We had lost the toss and on a typical flat Hove wicket we struggled for most of the morning session. Tony Murphy, our slightly portly Lancastrian seamer, bowled a bouncer to Alan Wells, who promptly dispatched it onto the dilapidated Sussex pavilion. When the ball came back, we could hardly believe what we saw in front of our collective eyes. The rough side had been so badly scuffed when it landed on the roof that the ball started to boomerang, reverse swing style.

Having spotted this, I suggested to Alec Stewart, the captain, it may be time for Bickers to have a bowl! Result? Bicknell took six wickets for not many and Sussex were bowled out for 240 on a flat wicket. Of course, I still needed to bowl well with the reverse swinging ball – but would I have been so successful had the ball not swung round corners? It would be honest to own up and say probably not. When the ball started to swing in the way it did, I suddenly became a much better bowler.

Curiously, events like that incident at Hove can have an effect on a player's career. At Hove, it did not seem to matter whether the wicket haul had been achieved by conventional methods, or reverse swing. I had been 'noticed'.

By 1990, when I was only 21 years old, cricket writers were mentioning my name for England selection. My performance in the first two games of the season had been unspectacular to say the least. Starting at Sussex, I ended the game with figures of 130-0, a disappointing performance in my first match of the year. Next game, against Lancashire at The Oval, we batted first and scored 707 all out. Lancashire then batted for over two days, scoring nearly 900 runs. My lacklustre figures totalled 170-1. After two games, I had taken 300-1. This was certainly not the form required of an England bowler. However, by the end of the year I had taken 65 wickets at an average of 25 apiece and was selected for the Ashes tour. How did this turnaround happen? I have to admit it was the arrival at Surrey of Waqar Younis!

Few people had heard of the young Waqar Younis from Pakistan when he arrived at Surrey and became my opening bowling partner. The ball reverse swung for most of that summer and with him scaring batsmen at one end, I cleaned up at the other. Chris Smith, the former England opener once said about Waqar: "You knew what was coming, but you couldn't do a thing about it." He was referring to the inswinging yorker, the sand shoe crusher.

On many occasions that year county teams reached somewhere around a 120-2, but were then bowled out for 200. My contribution to this was tight bowling at my end. That season I learned a lot about the art of bowling. For example, I bowled fuller when the ball swung and I learned when to attack and when to defend. Developing the art of reverse swing bowling under the tutelage of Waqar Younis was a memorable stage of my career.

The Waqar partnership had earned me a tour to Australia, but life turned out to be tough when I arrived there. The kookaburra balls didn't reverse swing and I had no one bowling the other end quite like Waqar. It was no real surprise to me that I struggled on that tour. I was not selected for any of the Test matches and I lost confidence. Worse, people lost confidence in me. I realised later I had been selected on the back of something that I couldn't replicate in Australia. In hindsight I needed to become a better bowler than I was at 21 years of age and to play for England in the future.

Waqar had arrived at Surrey with no reputation at all; hardly anyone had seen him bowl. He came on the recommendation of Imran Khan, who knew our then captain, Ian Greig. The first time I saw him was in the nets where he was terrorising several of our young batsmen. There and then a star was born. As no one outside the Surrey nets had seen him bowl, he was the unknown quantity, the X factor, we had been searching for. He devastated some of the early teams we played.

For instance, he clean bowled Ian Botham in a Sunday League game against Somerset with a ball that swung four feet and ripped out two stumps. Botham looked stunned as he walked off. He wasn't the only batsman that this happened to in Waqar's career. He was raw in the early stages, often struggling with the new ball and conceding a lot of runs. However, he was devastating with the old ball where he could control the swing brilliantly. When Waqar left Surrey and played for Glamorgan he started to swing the new ball as well, bowling outswingers at 90mph. It was no surprise when Glamorgan won the title that season.

Over the years Surrey have been at the centre of a few incidents that have drawn unfortunate attention to the club. In 1991 we were involved in a match at The Oval where I raised the quarter seam of the ball to help it reverse swing. I now admit it was stupid, but I did it to help me and the team. We got caught. Alec Stewart, our captain at the time, was summoned to the umpires' room and we were reported. I got off because no one pointed the finger at me. I was told quietly in the privacy of the Surrey dressing room not to do it again, because Alec would lose his job. We had to be careful after that. We were regarded with suspicion and sometimes accused of ball tampering when reverse swing took a heavy wicket toll.

Although no one was reported for a long time, some other players and officials continued to believe that we were scratching the ball when we had the opportunity. I can reveal now, in all honesty, that we were not cheating. We were just cleverer than most at getting the ball to reverse swing. We knew the drill; *keep one side dry and rough, soak the other side with sweat and let the aerodynamics take over*. We exploited it quite well. At times the pitch didn't allow the ball to reverse swing, but when it did we had the bowlers at our disposal to wreak havoc and this played a major role in our one-day successes with the white ball.

A game in 2005, however, put Surrey back in the dock. Nottinghamshire were the visitors to The Oval early in the season. Surrey got off to a poor start and were bowled out for just over 200 on a very flat pitch. Nottinghamshire, with my brother Darren Bicknell in particularly good form, took a liking to our attack and were cruising at 180-0. About this time the ball started to come under scrutiny from the umpires.

I had been fielding most of the time at third man and mid on so I was fairly oblivious to what was going on. However, two quick wickets with late swing from Rikki Clarke and Jimmy Ormond indicated to everyone that the ball had started to reverse. The umpires suddenly became more involved. They took another look at the ball and told Mark Ramprakash, our captain, that they were taking it off us.

They awarded Nottinghamshire five runs and we sensed we were in big trouble. Someone on our side had furtively opened up the quarter seam. It looked like it had wings. This was ridiculous and a really stupid thing to do. At the end of the day, the club wanted some answers from us and we had a meeting. I was disappointed when no one stood up and admitted responsibility.

The club didn't help the situation by promising they would fine and punish the individual heavily. After such a threat, any chance of someone owning up diminished rapidly. Individually, we were fuming. The player who did it was lying to his team-mates and there is nothing worse than that in my opinion.

Inevitably, the finger was pointed at Pakistani Mo Akram, which was unfair. His knowledge of reverse swing meant he had no need to butcher the ball in such a manner. Mo was not an idiot and would never have resorted to such crudity. Perhaps he had been put in the frame by someone who may have wanted him to take the wrap. If that was the case, it did not fool us. The person who butchered the ball didn't have much idea about what he was doing.

Team morale plummeted that season. We lost eight points, the club fined us heavily and it left a lingering sour taste. Personally, I didn't want to pay the fine. I hadn't committed any offence, yet the club wanted to take £1,500 off me for something I had no idea was even happening.

Meetings followed and I remember Mickey Stewart coming down to Tunbridge Wells where we were playing Kent. In the changing room the speculation was rife – what was going to happen? The ECB had threatened us with a 16-point deduction and stiff fines. We decided to have a meeting on the outfield at the end of the day's play. We would try to agree what we wanted to do and look at the options that might resolve the entire unfortunate incident so that we could move on with our season. Unfortunately, it did not work out in the way we hoped and lingered like a bad smell. We knew what our options were:

- accept the fine
- appeal against it
- barter with the ECB

At the end of this odd meeting on the pitch I had had enough. I walked off, leaving most of the rest of the team not knowing what we were going to do. Nothing was agreed or finalised to my knowledge and the matter festered. We were docked eight points and the issue of the fine was put aside. No one really knew if the club could even fine us. It wasn't until the end of the season that we noticed money had been taken out of our wages. We were incandescent with rage.

It was not so much the furtive deduction of the money that infuriated us. We felt that the club had failed the players in the way the issue had been handled. As a team we admitted there had been wrongdoing which had damaged the reputation of Surrey County Cricket Club, and we deeply regretted it. However, at no stage in the entire affair, did anyone from the senior staff at the club apologise to the players over their own poor handling of the situation.

I felt sorry for Mickey Stewart, a man I respected. Mickey was asked to find the culprit and deal with him. These were, of course, matters that should have been the responsibility of the management of the club. The Professional Cricketers' Association now became involved, so that we could be aware of our legal position. Our poor form towards the end of that season may have signified the manner in which we were preoccupied with events taking place off the pitch.

When lie detectors were threatened and even contacting the police mentioned, it was not surprising that the performance of the team dipped. Surrey eventually got relegated by less than the eight points that had been deducted. Even now, people are still 'gob-smacked' when we tell them that we still don't know who was responsible for the ridiculous ball tampering on that day. All I know is that it was one of the saddest episodes in the club's history and in the many years I was a servant of the club. However, as you will have read, those bad times were easily surpassed by many subsequent years of fulfilment and satisfaction.

# Martin Bicknell

# The English Game

Having been part of the English game for the last 21 years as a player I get a little tired of people running it down. If we get hammered by Australia, it's the fault of the counties for not producing enough good players. When England win Test series did you ever hear the commentators say it's a product of our good system? The counties are an easy target. If you lose, look around for a scapegoat and there in front of you is the county system. Now, I am not saying our system is flawless but it produces more good things than bad. In recent times players like Alistair Cook, Ian Bell, Monty Panesar and Andrew Strauss have come into the Test side and performed straight away. Why is that? Is it because the standard of cricket in England is good? You don't often hear overseas players criticising the standard of our game, most are very complimentary. Occasionally you hear noises from sacked Australian coaches, but not from the players. It's time to stand up for our game.

One of the best ideas in recent times has been the introduction of two divisions. For many years, with just one division where all the teams played each other, teams could simply go through the motions at the back end of a season. If you are not challenging for silverware in late August what incentive do you have for winning the game? What incentive do you have to play competitive, hard cricket? The introduction of two divisions has taken away this comfort zone and we now play harder cricket, over the whole of the season. Promotion and relegation have put an end to the meaningless game. All games now have an edge that probably wasn't there before. You are either trying to go up or saving yourself from going down. I should know. I have played at both ends of the divisions. I am sure this has contributed to the improvement in our national side. Sure, we got beaten by Australia, but then everybody does. We are ranked second in the world as I write this, not bad for an underachieving side. One of the things I would like to see change though is the bonus points structure. As it stands at the moment you can draw a game and get 12 points. The most points you can get for winning a game is 22. You can actually win a game and only get 16 points. This needs to be looked at. Teams need to be encouraged to go for the win more and not play 'safe' cricket.

The game changes on a yearly basis and what is right now may not be right in 10 years' time. When I first started in 1986, the 40-over version of the game was very popular on a Sunday afternoon, attracting large crowds. Now there is hardly any cricket at weekends as we have switched to the more commercial weekdays to make money. Floodlit cricket has come to the fore. Counties are installing their own floodlights and early evening cricket is catching on. I hear a lot of people say that county cricket doesn't attract many watchers. Times have changed somewhat since the Fifties. People have far busier working lives and there is more competition for our free time than there ever was before. We have to make the game as entertaining as possible to retain our market share. That is why I believe Twenty20 cricket has been so successful. It captures the imagination better than other activities, and still represents value for money.

# Martin Bicknell

The game changes in other ways too, like the way it is played. In a 40-over game of cricket, opening the bowling was generally best for the bowler. If you bowled well you wouldn't expect to go for more than 20-25 runs off your eight overs, even on a good wicket. Teams would try to keep wickets in hand and a score of 200 was seen as very good. Nowadays, with fielding restrictions, opening the bowling can be the worst time to bowl. Teams have raised the scoring rates as expectations have grown. Scores in the 50-over form of the game have gone through the roof in recent years. Three hundred, previously an unbeatable score, is now considered quite gettable. Four hundreds have been scored and you have to wonder where it will all end. Will a team score 500 in the next 10 years? I think so. Scoring rates have increased in all forms of the game. It just goes to show that you are only limited in what you can do by what your brain tells you. If you believe you can score 400 in a day's cricket you can do it. Teams are doing it now in Test cricket. It is becoming normal to score at four an over, whereas before it was seen as far too adventurous. Again, where will it end?

As someone who is primarily a bowler, the game does seem loaded in favour of batting. And I have to admit, it's probably a good thing. All the law changes in recent times have come in to favour the batting side – one bouncer per over, free hit for a no ball, no balls counting for two, fielding restrictions, two close catchers, front foot no ball law changing and flat, straw coloured pitches. Name me one law change that has come in to help the bowlers? But spectators come to games to see big hitting and lots of runs scored. They don't pile through the gates to see me bowl a couple of maidens do they?

# BICKERS

I love the diversity of the county game. When I first started you would travel all around the country, play on a green wicket, then a dry, brown one that turns and then it might be on to a batting paradise for the next game, all in the space of a couple of weeks. I am sure this helped the development of young cricketers. It helped batsmen to appreciate the need to play in different ways and for bowlers to bowl in differing styles. In 1990 it all changed. Straw coloured wickets became the order of the day as the English Cricket Board wanted a universal playing surface. This was a huge mistake in my view. Cricket is played all around the world, in a variety of conditions. The pitches in India are vastly different to the ones in Australia, and the pitches in New Zealand are vastly different to the one in the West Indies. As young cricketers you need to further your education by playing on all types of surfaces. The best players will inevitably come to the fore as the guys with the correct techniques will always succeed.

Cricket has come a long way in this country but there is still room for a lot of improvement. The travelling we do as players before and after games is crazy, although it has improved markedly to when I first started. Back then you could play day one of the Championship match at The Oval on the Saturday, jump in your car after the day's play at 7.30pm, drive up to Yorkshire for a Sunday League game, and then drive back late Sunday night to restart the Championship match on the Monday. Madness! We would often be away for two weeks at a time, playing every day, travelling the length and breadth of England. It is a wonder there aren't more serious car crashes after a schedule like that. Driving back after a long day in the field is just asking for trouble. We do play a little less cricket these days and the scheduling has changed. Four-day matches are still followed by one-day games, often involving travel and no preparation. But with the amount we play there isn't really an alternative. A reduction of one, one-day competitions may help this and allow more time for preparation, training and recuperation.

The advent of Twenty20 cricket has been a revelation for the county game. When it first started Surrey made no allowance for it in their budget for making money. As players we were a bit sceptical, but there again, all players are that way inclined. We turned up for our first match against Middlesex at The Oval thinking 'this will either sink or swim' and we were blown away. A crowd of over 10,000 watched that game and since then things have only improved. The Oval is regularly sold out and matches at Lord's between us have always been full houses. The counties now rely on this money as part of their income and it has been a breath of fresh air for the county game. It has introduced a younger audience and more family orientated crowds. Hopefully it will have a knock on effect down the line. More people will play the game and in turn we will produce more cricketers. It is also no surprise the game has gone global. The ICC is never shy of trying to make money and this will also be a great money maker at international level. I hope though that the 50-over game doesn't suffer because of the success of Twenty20. We live in a society of instant entertainment and we must guard the longer form of the game.

We must also find a way of ensuring people can watch the game on their TVs. Sky taking over the coverage of the game will obviously have a detrimental effect on the numbers watching from home. However, I am a massive fan of Sky and what they have done for the game. When they started their coverage of England's tours back in 1990 there was virtually no interest from our national broadcasters in doing so. Sky brought overseas games live into our homes. It also started to cover more county cricket and would eventually show more England cricket. Now they cover Test and one-day cricket from all over the world. We can watch cricket in different countries all winter. Did the BBC ever do that? Do the BBC really want cricket back? Do Channel 4? It costs them too much money to buy the rights so they don't bid. Who can blame the ECB for going to the highest bidder? Cricket needs money to survive, but it also needs viewers, spectators and kids being brought up watching the game. It would be a great shame if they missed out. I hope somewhere down the line there is a compromise.

With all the money coming into the game I hope we can channel it in the right direction. Grass roots cricket is where you can really make a difference, not at the top end by giving it to counties to help fund their overseas players. The competition amongst counties has helped bring an influx of Kolpak players into our game. We are now in danger of spending too much money on non-qualified English players. However, we must not think that Kolpak players are the only problem. We have taken in many non-qualified players from different countries in the past. Players like Graeme Hick, Robin Smith, Kevin Pietersen and Allan Lamb, all top international cricketers and players who started out in this country as non-qualified Englishmen. So the problem isn't just the new influx coming in from South Africa. The problem lies with these players who are unsure which country they are going to pick to play for. Come over to England, play as a Kolpak player for a couple of years and then decide. That's just rubbish. Surely you know which country you want to play for? The other problem is with guys like Jacques Rudolph, coming over to England after playing regularly for South Africa and now becoming a local player. And now I hear Shane Warne is trying to become German so Hampshire can have another overseas player. How is that right?

We are very much limited in what we can do in this country with employment law. The ECB has implemented a system where clubs are penalised financially for fielding non-English qualified players, but is this really the solution? If we are not careful some of our up and coming players will have their route to the first team blocked by someone who doesn't want to play for our country. In an ideal world you would like your up and coming players playing the key roles in games. They should be the ones bowling the last overs in a one-day innings, batting to win the game, not your overseas players. If we can expose the younger players to pressure situations in these games they will learn quicker. I like the idea of overseas players, but they have to be of a standard that can help our younger players develop – much in the same way Waqar Younis was good for me at Surrey. But the 'ten a penny' South African wanting to make a quick buck on the side has no place in our game.

It's no coincidence that the best players in the game work the hardest. It happens in all sports. Tiger Woods has an incredible work ethic. David Beckham will spend hours on free kicks and for Jonny Wilkinson, there aren't enough hours in the day. So why is it a lot of our young cricketers don't work hard enough at their games? Do we have a culture in this country that breeds laziness? I can only speak as I find. I can give you two examples in recent years in the county game. Mark Ramprakash was an underachiever at international level, but possibly the hardest worker in the game. I have never played with anyone more dedicated to scoring runs than Ramps. No one practises better, and no one sells his wicket harder. Even if he is in the form of his life, he doesn't change his routine. First in the nets, practising the basics and grooving his shots.

Andy Flower is the other example. We played Essex a couple of years ago and Flower made one of the best hundreds you could ever wish to see. It was a turning wicket with plenty of bounce, Ian Salisbury was a real handful but Flower came out on top. He batted for over four hours on a hot day and ground it out. The next morning I got to the ground at 9am, a full hour before their warm-ups started. Who was in the nets with the coach? Andy Flower. It wasn't just a one off as I discovered. He is first to the ground every day, working on his game, trying to improve. Two examples of guys at the end of their careers.

There is no substitute for hard work. Look at Steve Harmison and Andrew Flintoff at various stages of their careers. After the 2003 season, Harmison, sensing there was something missing from his game, took himself off and trained with Newcastle before the winter tour. Footballers work a damn sight harder than cricketers and this shocked him. He discovered he could push himself to a new level and it was no coincidence he had a great tour of the Caribbean. Harmison became the best fast bowler in the world for a period of time. Flintoff was your typical young cricketer, very talented, but with a poor work ethic. Slightly overweight and not getting the most out of his ability he had to do something about it. Neil Fairbrother, the former Lancashire player and now his agent, sat him down and spelt out the facts to him. If he wanted to become a better cricketer his lifestyle had to change. He turned things around, worked hard, got fit, and changed the way he thought about cricket. He stopped 'playing' at the game and got serious. Surely there is a lesson for all young cricketers?

When I first started I was generally in the nets from 9am, bowling for a good half hour before warm-ups. I spent so much time with Geoff Arnold he must have been sick of the sight of me. I bowled after warm-ups too. There were days he would have to stop me bowling in case I had nothing left for the game. I worked hard, and I worked harder when things weren't going well too. As time moved on I cut down my bowling before the start of the game. It just isn't possible to carry on like that when you get older. I knew my game by then and knew what I had to do to play at my best. Towards the end of my career I did very little before the start of the day's play and I think this approach was copied by our youngsters at the club. They saw me doing very little and thought that was the way to go. They missed me grooving my action and working my nuts off to become a better bowler.

The bottom line is, you can tell someone what they should be doing to improve, but the ball is certainly in their court when it comes to doing anything about it. As Gary Player said, "the harder I work, the luckier I get".

The coaching side of the game fascinates me. I believe coaching is the biggest problem in the game. We can complicate the game to such an extent that we lose sight of what we are good at in the first place. There is no set method for delivering the ball in a straight line. The coaching book will tell you different, but how does that accommodate bowlers such as Lasith Malinga and Fidel Edwards? True, the best players in the world, McGrath, Pollock and Allan Donald do the simple things well. But where does that leave the unorthodox? Would an English coach have tried to change Muralitharan? I think so. It seems we try to make everyone bowl the same way, not look at what makes them good in the first place. I look at Liam Plunkett and see a robot, someone who looks so uncomfortable with his action. You need a certain amount of 'feel' as a bowler and at the moment he doesn't look as if he has any. I also believe there are a lot of coaches who try to justify their roles by trying to make changes in someone's action when it really isn't necessary. It's a fine line to get right, and most of the time we don't.

I also love the psychology of the game, the ability someone has to get inside your mind and make you think differently. This is where your county coach really earns his money. The gift to be able to bring out the best in a player is priceless. Ordinary county players have turned their games around on the back of more self belief. Finding the buttons to press in a player, and raising his game to the next level is an art form for any coach. Captains can do it too. Mike Brearley was probably the greatest example of a captain who could draw the best out of a player. Adam Hollioake was another in recent times. If you can make your players feel 10 feet tall, you are half-way towards creating a winning team.

Invariably I am asked about what it is like playing the game at the top level, and especially how much 'sledging' goes on. In this country there is a general respect for each other on the cricket field and no one really oversteps the mark. I have found it more prevalent at club level, where the amount of rubbish shouted at batsmen borders on the obscene. I don't know why it is worse at that level; do players think that is the way to play the game? Playing at that level I have often been embarrassed by what is being said. Does it make any difference to the batsman? When I was batting it just fired me up a bit more to succeed. If someone gave me a mouthful why would I want to get out? Why not infuriate them a bit more by batting longer? I didn't go in for it myself too often. Geoff Arnold was always pushing me to be more aggressive in my early years but I just couldn't pull it off. I wasn't quick enough to scare people and I couldn't think quickly enough to say something detrimental to a batter. I preferred the Richard Hadlee technique of bowling a good ball and turning back to bowl the next before the batsman looked up at you. What does work on a batter though is subtle suggestions about their technique. Mentioning the fact that they might be slightly playing across the ball or the fact that they aren't moving their feet very well gets into their heads. I am sure it is more effective than standing two feet away calling them a wanker.

Some of the best sledges of all time bear repetition though: Glenn McGrath bowling to Eddo Brandes, the big Zimbabwean fast bowler. McGrath, after beating the bat on countless occasions loses his rag. "Why are you so effing fat?" Brandes in reply, "Because every time I shag your wife she gives me a biscuit." Surely the best comeback of all time?

And the other one that really stands out is, Shane Warne bowling to Jimmy Ormond at The Oval in 2001. Ormond, struggling to lay bat on the great man is sledged by Mark Waugh standing at slip. "You're rubbish" came the first comment from Waugh. In reply Ormond said: "I may be crap, but at least I am the best player in my family." Good lad.

# What Now?

At the end of the season I had a little time to reflect on my career and the move away from cricket and to a 'proper' job. My Testimonial had gone brilliantly, culminating in a lunch at the Porter Tun rooms in the city. We had over 600 people in that room. It was full to the rafters, and it made the event so special. As it was the last event I made sure all the people that had helped me over my 21 years in the game were there. All my family came and celebrated my final appearance as a Surrey player. In my speech I fought back the tears, I was so emotional. I thanked everyone from my Mum to the helpers doing the raffle. But I think I got it just about right, didn't forget anyone and left special thanks for Jacqui. Jacqui has been incredible for me. Although we have only been together for a couple of years she knows me inside out and what makes me tick. Our relationship is so strong. She is a very special lady and when I asked her to marry me it was one of the best decisions I ever made.

Special thanks also went to Barry Kitcherside, my chairman for the year. Barry helped me out during my Benefit year 10 years earlier and in the intervening years we have become good mates. He is one of my favourite people in the world, always supportive, always wanting to help out. Without his contribution to my year we wouldn't have raised half the money we did. I owe him big time.

# Martin Bicknell

Leaving Surrey didn't mean the end of my association with the club. Before I knew it I was elected onto the general committee, then the cricket committee, and finally onto the Surrey cricket review group. It is a perfect role for me; I can stay involved but a fair distance away from the playing side. Who knows what will happen in the future with regard to Surrey? I have been offered a couple of jobs around the country already but Surrey is where my heart is. I just couldn't imagine coaching another team. I also believe that when you stop playing you shouldn't go straight into coaching the side you played for. You need to get away and do something else. I would love to get involved again in some capacity eventually though, even if it were looking after some of the younger bowlers in a part-time role.

While you are still playing, at the back of your mind you are always thinking ahead and wondering what you can possibly do when you can't play any more. I knew I wanted a total break from the game. I had spent the last 21 years travelling around the country, staying in hotels and not being around enough for my girls. I wanted a break from that. David Ward, the former Surrey batsman had got himself a job at Whitgift School as head of cricket, before going on to become director of sport. He told me he had landed a great job and it was something that really appealed to me. A couple of years before I knew I was going to retire I wrote to around 30 schools offering my services. I had no idea what response I was going to get, if any. I had some nice letters back saying the job I was after was already filled by a former cricketer, that sort of thing. I had an interview at St John's School in Leatherhead, but they weren't really after a full-time position. It didn't look too good until I took a call from Bob Noble, the director of sport at Charterhouse School in Godalming. To be honest he was a little vague about the position that might be available, but we agreed to meet. Richard Lewis was the current cricket pro at the school but Bob suggested that he was looking to step down to work with the younger players, leaving a gap at the top. I outlined what I needed salary-wise and he left to discuss it with the headmaster. The other spanner in the works was the fact that I was still playing and couldn't start full time until October 2006. It wasn't a problem though as Richard Lewis kept the seat warm until I was ready.

It is a great job. Not only do I look after the cricket team but I also coach football and hockey. The school has a great diversity to its sport and that is what really appeals to me. I get an immense amount of joy from 'my' football team winning on a Saturday, and even from hockey, a sport I played once or twice when I was at school. The competitive fire still burns on.

At the end of 2006 I came out with a classic Steve Redgrave comment, "If anyone ever sees me near a cricket pitch again they can shoot me." I couldn't honestly ever see myself playing cricket again. My body was in pieces and my desire to play was zero. The school had other ideas. They persuaded me to play for the MCC against the school in the annual match. I had bowled a little in the nets but in truth the thought of playing didn't really excite me. In the game I managed to cobble together a few runs, and then got out to one of the boys, much to the team's pleasure. When it came to my time to bowl I once again had the overriding feeling of not making a fool of myself in front of the boys. Crazy how I can still feel nervous after 20 years in the game. I bowled a few overs and took a couple of wickets. I even enjoyed it a bit. With the first game out of the way I received invitations to a few more. The Professional Cricketers' Association have a Masters team and I reluctantly agreed to play a few games. Then Richard Thompson called to say his team could do with me to help them out. All of a sudden I had let myself in for quite a lot of cricket. Some people may find this hard to believe but I actually enjoyed playing again. It was good social cricket, nothing too serious and it was fun. Maybe playing the game professionally for over 20 years you lose that side of it. The game isn't too much 'fun' at the top level; there is a lot of pressure, as there should be. I didn't want to go down that route again, but I rediscovered my love of the game by just enjoying those days. I may even do it again.

I am still involved from my playing days with the Professional Cricketers' Association. I sit on an Advisory Board and I play the odd fixture and turn up for corporate events too. In my opinion the PCA has stepped in where the county cricket clubs should be. They look after the former players in the game, provide a huge range of benefits to its members and are always on hand to offer advice. They have overhauled the pension system for cricketers, they provide training during and after players' careers and also financial assistance for training courses. But the biggest thing they have done is set up a benevolent fund for cricketers who have fallen on hard times. They have supported many ex-players and their families in times of trouble and will continue to do so. They are a progressive association and I am pleased to be helping them out. The county cricket clubs do very little when it comes to looking after their current and former players. I guess we are just employees in the grand scheme of things, and once we leave the club can wash its hands of you. It's a good job we have the PCA.

# BICKERS

Probably the best thing I have done since leaving the game is appear on 'Heartbeat' the popular television programme on Sunday nights. A friend of a friend enquired if I was available for three days' filming on the Yorkshire moors, playing a cricketer from down south. Fortunately it didn't involve me saying too many lines, just bowling a few balls and standing in the right place at the right time. It was great fun though. Three days on the Yorkshire moors being treated like a film star, but hard work too. Filming can take ages. Different angles and retakes make it a long day, especially as one scene involved me bowling at a set of stumps repeatedly until they had enough footage to do a little montage of me running through the middle order. As I have explained in this book already, bowling at the stumps is not something I am used to doing so it took some time. And just for fun the director thought it would be a good idea to get a stump camera in the middle stump for me to hit. It was nearly dark before I hit it once.

The basis of the story involved two teams playing for the local Cup. I was the 'ringer' from down south coming up to Yorkshire to win the game for the 'enemy'. The game was going well for my team until the local barmaid came out to bat; yes, the barmaid. She proceeded to reverse sweep me for four – not the first time it has happened but definitely the first time by a girl. Well that's how it looked on television; it took several hundred takes before she made contact with an underarm lob. The final scene involved an inebriated mechanic staggering out to bat needing six to win. Yes you guessed it. He hit me over extra cover and over the pavilion to win the game. Now we had a bit of a problem filming this scene. I had to bowl the ball and he just had to make contact. They could 'make up' the rest and show the ball flying over the pavilion with clever filming. I must have bowled 20 balls at him and he couldn't make contact at all. We were all beginning to die of hypothermia it was so cold. Then, out of nowhere he hit the ball. Not just a few yards either, he cleared the pavilion some 80 yards away. I looked stunned and it made for great TV.

I had a great time but I am not sure I will ever make a film star. It got pretty boring at times waiting for your scene to film. Add in the cold – they film all year up there – and it really wouldn't be my cup of tea. Great experience though.

Being retired I thought I could make a genuine run at getting down to be a 'scratch' golfer. So far I am a little way off. I have got down to two but the elusive 'scratch' seems a long way off. I have been obsessed by the game since I was 18 and it has given me a great release from the pressures of cricket. I can think of nothing better to do than play golf with your mates on a warm sunny afternoon. I am sure a few of my ex-team-mates thought I loved golf more than cricket. They had a point at times. I did seem to have the odd injury that prevented me from playing cricket but still allowed me to play golf, but golf will always come a close second.

Although I have ambitions to become a scratch golfer I would never want to play the game professionally. The pressure these guys are under to hole a nasty four-foot putt is way too much for me. Part of the reason I love the game so much is that I am under no pressure to succeed. That is when the fun goes out of it for me. I do play in various different 'Opens' around Surrey and it is great when you play well and get involved in the prizes. However, the day when I take it too seriously is the day I will have to stop.

Across the sports there are many people I admire. In golf, the obvious players like Tiger Woods, Nick Faldo and Seve Ballesteros would be most people's choices. Perhaps the odd one out would be John Daly. Daly burst onto the scene in 1991 winning the PGA of America at Winged Foot. Daly was seventh reserve for that event, hadn't even seen the course before, but went out without any fear of failure and ripped it up. His style of 'grip it and rip it' is very refreshing for any golfer. It looks as though he doesn't have any nerves at all the way he plays, and always takes the positive option. Faldo I loved watching. At his peak there wasn't a better tactician in the game. He would plot his way around the course with the precision of a surgeon. Such a contrast from Daly, but both in their own way are people I enjoy watching. But the man is obviously Tiger. Never in the game can one man have been so far out in front of any other player. He is the supreme champion, never faltering when under pressure, always coming up with the shot when it is needed. His coolness under the intense pressure of a 'major' is something that all sportsmen aspire to. We all strive to perform under pressure, to come out on top when others fall by the wayside. He does it time and time again; there is no weakness in him as there so often is in others.

I also love my football. Being a Leeds Utd fan I haven't had too much to smile about in recent years. I started supporting them in the early Seventies, when the Revie era was in full swing. I didn't really have a local side to go and watch so I chose Leeds, they were the best side around, and in my eyes they still are! We will be back, mark my words.

I love football in general, but there are areas of the game that I really don't like. The theatrical diving of the players is one thing but the hypocrisy of the people involved is something else. The managers are mostly to blame. Just recently Chelsea were awarded a penalty against Liverpool, clearly the worst decision of all time, but a penalty. Chelsea scored, got a draw, and Jose Mourinho 'didn't get a clear view of the incident'. A game later, Chelsea were denied a goal by a referee and Mourinho goes ballistic and blames the ref for his side not winning. Didn't hear him mention the fact they should have lost at Liverpool the week before. Surely everyone can see through this? The hypocrisy is just too much for me sometimes. I know these guys are under a lot of pressure, but please, can we have a level of understanding that decisions even out over time? I guess it's a bit like a batsman complaining about a poor decision he has just received and forgetting about the poor decision that went in his favour in the previous game. I would love a football manager to come out and say just once that his team were lucky to win the game, and the referee had a good game. Wishful thinking I know, but wouldn't it be nice?

Since I left the game I have of course become a better player, it goes with the territory. And in 10 years' time I will have become better still. Again it's just logic. I will forget the bad days and leg stump half volleys; never would I have bowled a short wide ball either. It's a bit like when you look back at your youth and only remember the sunny days. Rainy days are consigned to the back of your memory bank; they didn't happen. The game evolves. But if you listen to some of the old players, cricket is the only game that hasn't made any progress at all. All the other sports have made giant strides. People run faster, jump higher and throw further. In cricket, the game stands still, apparently. It's all rubbish really. Sure there were great players 50 years ago, even 25 years ago, but the game moves on. Players are better now than they were back then, and they will be better still in 20 years' time. I love watching old clips of cricket and the way the game was played. I have great respect for the traditions of the game, and I love the history around the game. But please don't tell me the game was better back then. It's just not true.

I am often asked "who was the best batsman you bowled against?" and "who was the best bowler you faced?" It is a very difficult question for a number of reasons. I bowled at many great players, sometimes with success and sometimes not so well. I didn't particularly like bowling at batsmen who looked to pull anything just back of a length, so someone like Aravinda Da Silva, the brilliant Sri Lankan could be a nightmare to bowl to. In the same bracket I would put Brian Lara. Bowl a fraction short to him and watch it sail over deep square leg. On the other hand there are batsmen who just don't look like getting out and that can cause its own set of problems. Rahul Dravid, David Boon and Steve Waugh fall into that bracket. I didn't mind bowling to them, for if you bowled well they respected it and didn't look to dominate you. Although I haven't done it that often I am sure I wouldn't like to bowl to Kevin Pietersen. I did get him out once but in that short time he threatened to take me apart. You have to be at the top of your game to compete at that level. So, in short, there are guys who dominate and others who are content to bat for long periods of time and not give you a sniff. If I had to pick one though, it would be Brian Lara. He could play any way he chose.

Bowling-wise, there are some nasty fast bowlers out there who I am sure fancied bowling at me. Courtney Walsh would be right up there as the hardest to face – awkward bounce and the feeling that he always had a ball up his sleeve that could hit you on the head. And he did, straight on the visor, before I could blink. The obvious greats like Hadlee and Marshall were incredible exponents of the art of seam bowling. Both were great at working batsmen out, highly skilled with an ability to get something out of even the flattest pitch. For spin bowlers there are two that stand out, Warne and Muralitharan. Warne never really stood out when he played for Hampshire, saving his best for Australia. Murali was just impossible to score off, an incredible mixture of deliveries and right-angled spin. But my vote for hardest to face would be Malcolm Marshall. Just that bit quicker than Hadlee, but I learnt an awful lot about the art of seam bowling from both of them.

The other question that I am frequently asked is, what was the best team and players I played with at Surrey? At the risk of upsetting a few people here goes: I will pick two overseas players and I will be twelfth man.

Mark Butcher

Alec Stewart (wicket-keeper)

Mark Ramprakash

Graham Thorpe

Alistair Brown

Adam Hollioake (captain)

Chris Lewis

Alex Tudor

Ian Salisbury

Saqlain Mushtaq

Waqar Younis

Not a bad team, although I am sure there will be a couple of disappointed people out there reading this, my brother for one, Jon Batty and Ian Ward. It was a tough call between Sylvester Clarke and Waqar but Waqar edged it on his ability to destroy sides in one spell. Saqi obviously gets the vote and he would probably be the best player I have ever played with. Chris Lewis wins the battle of the all rounders without ever really fulfilling his potential at Surrey. The choice of two spinners is crucial to my side; Ian Salisbury has taken a fair amount of stick from Surrey supporters over the years. However, he was crucial to the success of the side and gave us the X factor, someone who could take you a wicket from nowhere. I am sure you can gather from the rest of the book who was my favourite captain to play under, so that needs no explanation. The rest are fairly self-explanatory. Alex Tudor may be the only other contentious decision. It's true he has never taken 50 wickets in a year, and of course injuries held him back over his career, but on any given day he could be a nightmare to bat against. Extracting steep bounce with good pace, he was a handful on most pitches.

Don't ask me to pick a side to play against; there are just too many good players out there.

As I was coming to the end of my career I gave great thought to how I wanted to be remembered in the game. Was it that I wanted to be remembered as someone who won trophies and had a good career record? Or was it someone who gave everything for their side, made the most out of their ability and was a good bloke to play with. I choose the latter; it is so important to me to be remembered the right way. I loved my time in the game, most of the people I played with and the fun we had. It had its fair share of disappointment along the way, and too big a share of tragedy for anyone. But I loved it; it was the best time of my life.